T0329135

Cambridge Elements ☰

Elements in World Englishes
edited by
Edgar W. Schneider
University of Regensburg

POSTHUMANIST WORLD ENGLISHES

Lionel Wee
National University of Singapore

CAMBRIDGE
UNIVERSITY PRESS

University Printing House, Cambridge CB2 8BS, United Kingdom

One Liberty Plaza, 20th Floor, New York, NY 10006, USA

477 Williamstown Road, Port Melbourne, VIC 3207, Australia

314–321, 3rd Floor, Plot 3, Splendor Forum, Jasola District Centre, New Delhi – 110025, India

79 Anson Road, #06–04/06, Singapore 079906

Cambridge University Press is part of the University of Cambridge.

It furthers the University's mission by disseminating knowledge in the pursuit of education, learning, and research at the highest international levels of excellence.

www.cambridge.org
Information on this title: www.cambridge.org/9781108964906
DOI: 10.1017/9781108990615

First published 2021

A catalogue record for this publication is available from the British Library.

ISBN 978-1-108-96490-6 Paperback
ISSN 2633-3309 (online)
ISSN 2633-3295 (print)

Posthumanist World Englishes

Elements in World Englishes

DOI: 10.1017/9781108990615
First published online: April 2021

Lionel Wee
National University of Singapore
Author for correspondence: Lionel Wee, ellweeha@nus.edu.sg

Abstract: A posthumanist approach problematizes the separateness and centrality of humans in understanding the world around them. Posthumanism does not deny the role of humans but questions the assumption that it is human activity and agency that should be given pride of place in any analysis of social activity. This carries important and interesting implications for the study of world Englishes, some of which are explored in this Element. Sections 3 and 4, respectively, explore posthumanism in relation to two specific topics in world Englishes, creativity and language policy. These topics have been chosen because they allow us to see the contributions that posthumanism can make to a micro-level (creativity) as well as macro-level (language policy) topic.

Keywords: agency, assemblage, creativity, global English, mobile policy

ISBNs: 9781108964906 (PB), 9781108990615 (OC)
ISSNs: 2633-3309 (online), 2633-3295 (print)

Contents

1 Regimes of Truth in the Study of Language

1.1 Introduction

The study of language has often drawn on notions that tend to be understood from a human-centric perspective. A notion such as agency, not to mention the related ones of creativity and competence in language use, are all typically understood as stemming from the goals and desires of human actors. It is humans who have agency, it is humans who are creative and it is humans to whom competence in language use can be meaningfully attributed. Language is conceptualized as a medium, perhaps the primary medium, through which these notions are exercised and manifested.

Which brings us to yet another notion: that languages exist as identifiable and distinct varieties such as 'English', 'Singlish' and 'Hawaiian Creole English'. Here, too, the human-centric perspective persists. These varieties are defined in terms of their affiliation with particular human communities (e.g. 'native speakers', 'learners', 'migrants', 'colonizers').

Thus, when claims are made about how to understand or analyse linguistic behaviour, the reliance on these notions – with their anthropocentric interpretations – makes it 'obvious' that we are looking at activities that are fundamentally human in orientation. Even when not explicitly highlighted in discussions about language, these notions are nevertheless usually in the background. Consequently, they go on to inform the kinds of conclusion that can be considered 'sensible'.

There is at work here a 'regime of truth', where what counts as true is the result of an institutionalized series of practices that regulate the production, distribution and circulation of statements (Foucault 1977: 14). In the case of the study of language, current academic orthodoxy makes it almost unthinkable to question the anthropocentric orientation involved (although see Pennycook 2018).

The goal of this section is to make the case that there are serious problems with this anthropocentric stance. The next section then outlines an alternative approach, described as posthumanism (Barad 2007; Bennett 2010; Pennycook 2018). And the sections that follow focus on specific implications of posthumanism for the study of world Englishes. To clarify, the aim is not to trivialize or dismiss the role of human actors. Rather, the objective is to better understand the place of human activity in relation to language without assuming as a default or as axiomatic that human practices must take pride of place as the source of how language is being manifested or how it is to be analysed.

This might suggest that we are merely replacing one regime of truth with another. But the shift to newer regimes of truth is neither trivial nor a simple matter of substitution. It is hard won given the entrenched status of orthodoxies and the concomitant difficulties involved in reconceptualizing what has heretofore been taken as 'common sense'. More importantly, it is something that must be attempted not least because the current regime of truth is problematic. In the next section, I touch on two such problems, one relating to agency and the other relating to communities and language varieties.

1.2 Cracks in Current 'Truths' about Language

1.2.1 Agency

The matter of agency has long bedevilled social theorists. There have been proposals that the locus of agency lies within the individual, in human-created and inherited social structures or that it emerges from some kind of dialectic between the two (Bourdieu 1977; Giddens 1984; Goffman 1956; Parsons 1937; Simmel 1976). These proposals all share the idea that agency must have some localizable human fount, an idea that the study of language in society has taken on board as well.

For example, in an influential and critical discussion of agency in language policy, Tollefson (1991) distinguishes between the neoclassical and historical-structural approaches. The neoclassical approach emphasizes the rational and individualistic nature of choices. As an illustration, individuals may choose to learn a new language because of certain perceived benefits such as access to a better job. Or they may decide that the time and money spent on learning a new language may not be worth the potential benefits and hence they may not make the effort to expand their linguistic repertoire. Whatever the outcome, the neoclassical approach treats these as decisions that are freely, rationally and individually made.

The historical-structural approach, in contrast, emphasizes inherited constraints and resources. For example, in a society in which English is the medium of instruction, a student from a minority ethnic community and whose home language is not English will face different challenges in doing well scholastically than someone whose home language is also English will. Such a situation is faced by Vietnamese migrants to America (Tollefson 1991). Adult migrants are required to attend English-language classes while juggling these classes with work and trying to acculturate to a new society. Their children, too, face social and linguistic adaptation challenges in school. The difficulties and problems faced by them cannot be dismissed as being due to individual laziness or lack of discipline – as they would be under the neoclassical approach.

From a language policy perspective, the neoclassical approach assumes that successes or failures in language policy can and must be laid at the feet of the individual. The historical-structural approach, by way of contrast, gives greater attention to how macro-social and historical forces need to be considered as contributing to the differential distribution of privileges and handicaps. The major differences between the two approaches are summarized by Wiley (1996: 115):

- The unit of analysis employed: While the neoclassical approach focuses on individual choices, the historical-structural pays attention to relationships between groups.
- The role of the historical perspective: The neoclassical is more interested in the current language situation; the historical-structural, in contrast, emphasizes the role of sociohistorical factors.
- Criteria for evaluating plans and policies: The neoclassical is primarily amoral in its outlook; policies are evaluated in terms of how efficiently they achieve their goals. The historical-structural is more sensitive to the issue of domination, exploitation and oppression.
- The role of the social scientist: Consistent with its amoral outlook, the neoclassical assumes that the social scientist must and can approach language problems in an apolitical manner. In contrast, the historical-structural views political stances as inescapable so that 'those who avoid political questions inadvertently support the status quo'.

Tollefson's distinction between the two approaches is intended to raise questions such as 'Why must that individual expend those particular costs?'; 'Why are those particular benefits rather than others available to that individual?'; 'What are the costs and benefits for other people in the community?' (1991: 32). Tollefson's position is that the neoclassical approach has been all too dominant. Countering this with the historical-structural approach would instead shift the focus to examining 'the historical basis of policies and to make explicit the mechanisms by which policy decisions serve or undermine particular political and economic interests' (Wiley 1996: 32).

Although Tollefson's distinction makes important points, problems still remain. Positioning the issue of agency as a series of dichotomies – between individual and group, between the ahistorical and the historical, between the apolitical and the political – retains the assumption that agency has an identifiable human locus, either individual or group, with Tollefson coming down in favour of the latter.

More recently, but in a similar vein, Spolsky (2009) has called for attention to be given to language management. It is certainly not unreasonable to talk about language management since there are clearly attempts by various authorities (parents, teachers, politicians, etc.) to influence the language practices of targeted populations (children, students, communities). Where this kind of talk becomes problematic, however, is when we assume that the agency of management is isolatable and can be unequivocally identified, as Spolsky (2009: 6; emphasis added) seems to propose:

> Management ... is not automatically successful. It presupposes a manager ... *As a rule, I will take the position that it is management only when we can identify the manager.*

The idea of an identifiable manager again involves the assumption that there is a definable locus of human agency and it returns us to the problems that plagued Tollefson's distinction between the neoclassical and the historical-structural. But trying to identify the manager in this way raises complicated questions about agency such as the following (Ahearn 2001: 8):

> Can agency only be the property of an individual? What types of supra-individual agency might exist? ... Similarly, we might also be able to talk about agency at the sub-individual level ... thereby shedding light on things like internal dialogues and fragmented subjectivities? ... Another avenue for potential research involves investigating theories of agency that people in other cultures or speech communities might espouse ... Who do they believe can exercise agency?

Such complications arise because even a body such as 'the government', 'the ministry' or 'the community' is really an abstraction over multiple sub-entities (themselves potentially recursively sub-dividable) so that 'internal dialogues and fragmented subjectivities' apply no less to organizations and groups than they do to individuals. Once this is recognized, then it is important to acknowledge that any attempt at identifying the language manager can be controversial and complex, not least because there are also often culture-specific beliefs about what kinds of entity can exercise agency, the manner in which such agency is exercised and the nature of the evidence considered relevant in diagnosing the activity of an agent.

In addition to the distributed nature of agency, there is another problem. This is the tendency to downplay if not dismiss the roles of non-human entities. Yet, as Bennett (2010: 34) observes:

> No one really knows what human agency is, or what humans are doing when they are said to perform as agents. In the face of every analysis, human agency remains something of a mystery. If we do not know just how it is that human agency operates, how can we be so sure that the processes through which nonhumans make their mark are qualitatively different?

A good illustration of what Bennett means is provided by Latour (Hazard 2013: 66; emphasis added):

The theorist and anthropologist Bruno Latour – whose 'network' from actor-network theory is for our purposes a concept loosely equivalent to 'assemblage' – represents this idea with exceptional clarity in his analysis of a central claim of the National Rifle Association (NRA) (1999: 176–80). According to Latour, the NRA's braying insistence that 'guns don't kill people, people kill people' is premised on more anthropocentric understandings of agency that treat material things such as guns as diligent *instruments of human volition*. Latour contends, on the contrary, that once a person picks up a gun, she or he is not quite the same person as before. Guns, among other things, when connected with humans, make up *new networks or assemblages that embolden or enable certain kinds of actions*, specifically, killing. (One would not use the barrel of a gun to arrange a bouquet of roses, after all.) A shared human recognition of the gun's violent potential – drawn from, say, the news and films – induces an affective reaction on the part of the holder, who might feel powerful and dangerous. The physical heft of the gun and the contours and textures of its surfaces may reinforce such feelings and accentuate an inclination to violence. Its trigger, which is shaped to accommodate a finger, directs human activation of a bullet. And, of course, the speed of the bullet enables a murder far more easily than if one set out to kill with his or her bare hands. According to Latour, when a person kills with a gun, it is not only the person who kills. It is the larger assemblage that kills. Its murderous agency is distributed across its many parts including a finger, a trigger, a bullet, a human brain, violent films, and so on. *Agency is always complex agency, unlocalizable and distributed across assemblages of both humans and things.*

Latour's example neatly illustrates the problem with restricting agency to human actors such that non-human entities are seen as mere 'instruments of human volition'. However, the person who is holding a gun has agency in a way that is different than a person not holding gun – even if both have the desire or intention to kill. The combination 'person + gun + intention to kill' constitutes a new network or assemblage that allows for some types of action over others. Taking this insight seriously means recognizing that agency is not only 'unlocalizable'; it is also 'distributed across assemblages of both humans and things'.

'Assemblage' (Deleuze and Guattari 1987) is a technical concept with major implications for the study of language. This is because an assemblage can be made up of a highly diverse and ad hoc set of elements and it has no central organizing agent (Bennett 2010: 23–4). One of the things that the next section will discuss is what it means to think of language as an assemblage. For now, I move on to the second problem with the current regime of truth.

1.2.2 Communities and Language Varieties

In a critical survey of the sociological roots of sociolinguistic theorizing, Williams (1992) points out that sociolinguistics has largely taken on board the structural functionalist idea of society as a complex system with mutually dependent parts that work together harmoniously (Durkheim 1933; Parsons 1971). As he (Williams 1992: 228) explains:

> This social system, despite its internal diversity, was conceived of as an integrated whole. Integration was associated with the idea of social equilibrium. A society in a state of equilibrium was one devoid of conflict, with every member knowing what was expected of him/her in any role, and where such expectations were constantly met.

Language, in this conception, is 'merely a mirror of society ... not so much social, as a representation of the social' (Williams 1992: 231). Such a view of language served the purpose of establishing sociolinguistics in the early days as a distinctive field of inquiry, allowing the field, as Blommaert (2016: 243) observes, to emphasize 'clear, distinct, and stable units that can become sociolinguistic units: the speech community, the dialect or language area, and language (or dialect, sociolect, etc.) itself'. As a reflection of a structural functionalist conception of society, these sociolinguistic units also emphasized shared understandings and consensus. Differences and conflicts were either of minor interest or seen as signalling the transition to a new equilibrium.

This view of language and its relation to society has, in recent times, come under scrutiny. Consider phenomena such as globalization and language contact, both of which have significance when studying how language varieties emerge. Globalization is all too often treated as a primarily economic phenomenon (Perrons 2004: 35–54; Wade 2001) even though it is, in fact, a highly multidimensional set of processes that also include the political, technological and cultural (Giddens 2002: 10; Kennedy 2001: 8). The key characteristic of globalization is, as Giddens (1990: 64) points out, 'the intensification of worldwide social relations which link localities in such a way that local happenings are shaped by events occurring many miles away and vice versa'. This intensification is facilitated (some might even say 'exacerbated') by developments and advances in communication and transportation technologies that allow individuals and communities to more easily maintain contact with multiple groups across the globe.

As far as language contact is concerned, this means that it is not only people who are mobile and who therefore bring with them their language practices as they move from one place to another. Languages, too, can move, even without speakers, since media technologies also allow for the relatively rapid and widespread dissemination of language resources – in the form of what we might think of as cultural texts – through processes of spamming, streaming and downloading as well as, of course, the more traditional media of radio, movies and television. The dissemination of popular culture, for instance, is not so much via interactions between groups of speakers as it is about how speakers come to appropriate culturally transmitted words and phrases as a result of textually mediated encounters through social media and various streaming services.

However, the traditional focus in language contact studies has tended to be informed by the assumption that different language types (e.g. pidgins, creoles) arise as bounded groups of speakers come to interact with one another. Even outside contact situations, trying to rely on specific community types to anchor varieties of language has proved problematic. Early references to 'language community' (Laitin 2000) were replaced by 'speech community' (Labov 1972) and the latter itself became contentious because of the need to acknowledge the 'plurilingual' nature of any community (Silverstein 1996).

The movements of people and language resources, then, raise interesting challenges and issues for our contemporary understanding of language, requiring a rethink of those assumptions that sociolinguistics has inherited. Where the movement of people is concerned, mobility no longer necessarily means loss of contact with the home community. For example, the time that a migrant spends living and working in the host community need not result in a reduction in the frequency of interactions with friends and family members back home. There is actually no single homogeneous entity that we can meaningfully describe as 'the migrant', since the relevant factors that influence a person's decision to migrate are extremely varied. Faist (2000: 37) gives us a sense of just how varied these factors can be, when he notes that they:

> may be related to improving and securing: wealth (e.g. income), status (e.g. prestigious job), comfort (e.g. better working and living conditions), stimulation (e.g. experience, adventure, and pleasure), autonomy (e.g. high degree of personal freedom), affiliation (e.g. joining friends or family), exit from oppression of all kinds, meaningful life (e.g. improving society), better life for one's children, and morality (e.g. leading a virtuous life for religious reasons). In this view the potential migrant could not only be a worker, a member of a household or a kinship group, but also a voter, a member of ethnic, linguistic, religious, and political groups, a member of a persecuted minority, or a devotee of arts or sports.

The result of all this variation is what has sometimes been called 'superdiversity' (Vertovec 2007). As Blommaert and Rampton (2016: 22) point out, '[s]uperdiversity is characterized by a tremendous increase in the categories of migrants, not only in terms of nationality, ethnicity, language, and religion, but also in terms of motives, patterns and itineraries of migration, processes of insertion into the labor and housing markets of the host societies, and so on' (cf.

Vertovec 2010). The predictability of the category of 'migrant' and of his/her sociocultural features has disappeared. While it may have once been feasible to understand the impact of migration on language contact by identifying specific waves of migration patterns, it is not clear that such an approach would still be feasible under the conditions of late modernity (Rampton 2006).

Where the movement of language resources is concerned, the comments by Stroud and Prinsloo (2015: ix–x) are pertinent:

> Traditionally, studies of moving words have been filtered through bounded notions of language and community. From this perspective, linguistic forms are treated as belonging to (expert) speakers of the community, as displaying structural integrity and as being targets of acquisition by learners . . . But what if mobility, far from being an aberration or exception, is actually the normal state of affairs? What if instead of viewing linguistic mobility through the lens of a localist idea of language, the tables were turned and language was viewed through the lens of mobility? . . . Power geometries of language are at work when linguistic forms travel – some travel well and others not so well. When the places and spaces across which words move are 'filled with codes, customs, rules, expectations and so forth' (Blommaert 2005: 73) with their indexical orders, the significance and value of particular forms of language are recalibrated.

Thus, Heller (2008: 505) has highlighted 'the limits of the utility of fixed sociolinguistic or linguistic variables or of fixed correspondences between language (understood as a whole, bounded system), individual social position within stable communities, and community boundaries' in dealing with the flows, transformations and circulations of linguistic and other semiotic resources.

However, even these critiques of the relationship between language use and community do not go far enough in questioning the anthropocentric orientation that undergirds much of language studies. Consider the fact that language is becoming increasingly automated. It is undeniable that various technological advancements ranging from relatively simple computer programmes to highly developed artificial intelligence (AI) are increasingly involved in our use of language for communication.

Take, as just one example, the by now ubiquitous use of automated signs at carparks to indicate to drivers if a carpark is full and, if not, just how many empty lots are actually available. Thus, a driver who is approaching a carpark may, variously, encounter a sign that says 'Carpark full' or one that says, for instance, '86 lots available'. The automated sign at the entrance to the carpark is obviously intended to be communicative, having been programmed to take note of the number of cars that are already present in the carpark and to convey in real time the relevant information (i.e. how many lots are still empty) to drivers who may be thinking of parking their cars there. In a multi-storey carpark, drivers may even be told of how any empty lots available are actually distributed over the different levels (e.g. 'Level 3, 24', 'Level 4, 35').

This raises the question of how we are supposed to conceptualize the communicative act. Presumably we wish to avoid anthropomorphizing the carpark sign and thus to avoid attributing intentions to the sign. Nevertheless, we would still need to take a position on whether the Gricean Cooperative Principle with its related Maxims ought to be considered applicable. Does it make sense, for example, to assert that the machine is being cooperative, that it is perhaps observing the Maxim of Quality? And given that the machine has been programmed to convey information in a syntactically and lexically restricted manner, would we want to suggest that the brevity of its message shows that it is not in violation of the Maxim of Manner? And if our stance is instead that the Gricean Principle is not applicable, what then are the available conceptual alternatives?[1]

Certainly, we would want to acknowledge that whoever programmed and installed the machine intended it to be useful and that its usefulness includes conveying the relevant information in as brief and clear a manner as possible. So, Grice's ideas might be still applicable if we treat the communication as coming from the programmer. This position is not without problems of its own, however. Bringing in the programmer into the pragmatics of the carpark communication event so as to justify the applicability of Grice's ideas assumes that the programmer is yet another human being. Qua human being, it is then unproblematic to attribute to this entity the kinds of intention and goal ordinarily discussed in relation to Grice. However, in the case where some form of communicative technology has been created by a computer programme, then the same questions about how to understand the communicative pragmatics arise once again.

This latter scenario is not as farfetched as it seems because machines are already capable of writing their own code (Galeon 2017). As programmes get more sophisticated and autonomous (see the discussion below on chatbots), it becomes more difficult and less plausible to equate the intentions of a programme with those of its programmer. But if we separate the intentions of the programmer from the programme itself, do we still have any grounds for attributing intentions to the programme? And we do indeed need to separate the programmer from the programme. This is because the specific information that is being conveyed at any one time about the state of the carpark (e.g. the actual

---

[1] See Wee (under preparation) for a detailed discussion of these matters.

number of lots available at any particular date and time) is not something that the programmer is likely even to be aware of. The information is gathered and conveyed via programmed sensors that are independent of the programmer (which is, of course, the whole point of the programming).

Another example involves the concept of an echoborg. An echoborg is a person whose utterances and gestures are determined to varying degrees by the communications that originate from an artificial intelligence programme. An echoborg is a specific kind of cyranoid (the latter term is clearly inspired by Rostand's play *Cyrano de Bergerac*). A cyranoid is defined by Corti and Gillespie (2015: 30) in the following manner:

> A cyranoid is created by cooperatively joining in real-time the body of one person with speech generated by another via covert speech shadowing. The resulting hybrid persona can subsequently interact with third parties face-to-face.

As Corti and Gillespie (2015: 30) observe, 'naïve interlocutors perceive a cyranoid to be a unified, autonomously communicating person'. In the case of an echoborg, the artificial intelligence is joined with a human surrogate such that the latter then becomes the public and human face of the former. Lamb (2015) provides a succinct description of what might happen with echoborgs:

> AIs use human surrogates or 'echoborgs' to speak their words and socialize with humans. The living, breathing avatar simply recites the computer's words at the conference table, serving as a humanizing conduit for an inhuman will.

The interactional goal here is to give the illusion that one is communicating with a fellow human being when, in fact, the communication originates from an artificial intelligence. The human with whom one is apparently communicating is really working at the behest of the artificial intelligence. Echoborgs can be useful since some individuals might feel more comfortable if they think they are interacting with another human even though the kinds of information and advice they want is better and more efficiently provided by an artificial intelligence.

Regardless, this 'synching' of a human front with messages that are created by an artificial intelligence raises conceptual issues such as the nature of speakerhood. Who exactly is speaking under such a condition where the activity of speaking is distributed over more than one entity? Is it the human extension or is it the artificial intelligence; or is such a binary approach misguided? Even if we were to decide, say, that the human extension is properly the speaker, we would still need to explain how we intend to understand the role played by artificial

Challenging the idea that language is an autonomous and integrated system is the 'trans-super-poly-metro movement' (Pennycook 2016). While there are minor differences in how the individual terms are employed (e.g. 'translanguaging' has a strong pedagogical orientation and 'polylingualism' stresses the need to attend to individual linguistic features rather than whole languages), the commonalities are more predominant and, hence, the collective sense of a 'movement'. There is here a shared emphasis on how speakers appear to mix the resources associated with conventionally established linguistic varieties to such an extent that any presumption of an existing autonomous linguistic system must be met with scepticism.

However, the radicalness of this movement has been questioned (Edwards 2012; Pavlenko 2017). If all the movement is doing is challenging the idea of fixed and stable language boundaries, then these are ideas already anticipated by Harris's (1988) integrationism and Bakhtin's (1981) heteroglossia (Pennycook 2016: 207–8). In the absence of a clear and robust conceptual alternative, however, the systems approach remains a convenient and still influential default. Unfortunately, as things stand, the 'trans-super-poly-metro movement' does not quite provide this alternative because it does not address the following key question: If boundaries are being crossed in the course of language mixing, what is the theoretical status of such boundaries?

And there are good reasons why boundaries cannot simply be ignored. Speakers do think in terms of boundaries between languages as they calibrate their own linguistic practices and evaluate those of others, even if such boundaries are constantly shifting and being renegotiated. Also, it cannot be denied that speakers themselves acknowledge that some of their mixing practices would be considered transgressive in certain contexts and by certain audiences. This means that the cultural reality of the boundaries that separate linguistic varieties has to find some place in a sociolinguistic account of language behaviour. Indeed, language acquisition in multilingual contexts involves learning when mixing across conventionalized language boundaries is socially appropriate and when it is not (Lanza 2004; Matras 2009). Finally, it is also the case that such mixing can in time come to constitute a 'register/lect/ variety' of its own – which means that newer sociolinguistic boundaries are being erected.

The real issue, then, is not that boundaries are irrelevant. Rather, it is how they can theoretically co-exist with innovations and changes and, moreover, in a way that also accommodates the flow, circulation and mobility of language and other resources. This is why the question of just what kind of 'thing' language is requires serious consideration (Blommaert (2010: 13; emphasis added):

Old and established terms such as 'codeswitching', and indeed even 'multi-lingualism', appear to rapidly exhaust the limits of their descriptive and explanatory power in the face of such highly complex 'blends' . . .

And not only that: *the question of where the 'stuff' that goes into the blend comes from, how it has been acquired, and what kind of 'competence' it represents, is equally difficult to answer.* Contemporary repertoires are tremendously complex, dynamic and unstable, and *not* predicated on the forms of knowledge-of-language one customarily assumes, since Chomsky, with regard to language.

As we see below, thinking of language as an assemblage affords significant advantages over the view of language as an autonomous bounded system. It provides a coherent account of regularities and fluidities in language while also being open to the idea of what actually constitutes 'the linguistic'.

2.4 The Assemblage

Deleuze and Guattari (1987: 406) tell us that an assemblage is a contingent mix of practices and things, where this contingent ensemble of physical and non-physical objects – broadly characterizable as 'semiotic' – is distinguished from yet other contingent ensembles in being 'selected, organized, stratified' and hence demarcated from an otherwise endless flow of circulating signs. Drawing also on Deleuze and Guattari, Bennett (2010: 23) succinctly describes assemblages as 'ad hoc groupings of diverse elements, of vibrant materials of all sorts'.

It therefore needs to be emphasized that assemblages can be organized and ordered, but also that this organization and order is contingent and changeable. The significant advantage of thinking in terms of an assemblage, then, is that it recognizes the role that boundedness plays in ontology, even as it at the very same time insists that we acknowledge that the boundaries can be multiple, contested and shifting. So, even though assemblages are always in the process of 'coming together and moving apart' (Wise 2005: 77), this does not mean that at a given point in time, there is neither structure nor order to them. But it does mean it is futile to try attributing agency to any specific member of the assemblage. Returning to Latour's example (section 1) of a person with a gun, there are multiple and changing assemblages depending on whether the person is holding the gun or whether the gun is stored in a safe away from the person. These different assemblages ('person + gun' or 'gun + safe' or even 'person + safe') involve different arrangements of entities with the potential for bringing about different effects.

As 'ad hoc groupings of diverse elements' (Bennett 2010: 23; see earlier), assemblages are therefore consistent with posthumanism's criticism of the assumption that entities – of whatever sorts – should be seen as having stable interiors and exteriors. And because assemblages have no central mechanism (Bennett 2010: 23–4), they are further consistent with posthumanism's scepticism about agency as having an identifiable locus.

Let us now consider three specific properties of assemblages that will be useful in developing our understanding of the linguistic assemblage.

2.5 Three Things to Note about Assemblages

The first thing to appreciate about assemblages is that signs (linguistic or otherwise) are both material and able to trigger other signs into self-organizing. In developing their ideas about assemblages, Deleuze and Guattari are cognizant of work in complexity theory,[3] which shows that some physical and biological systems can be triggered by environmental factors into self-organizing. This is an insight that Deleuze and Guattari take seriously but they do so by emphasizing the historical and political dimensions of complex systems (Bonta and Protevi 2004: 4):

> Signs are no longer limited to linguistic entities that must somehow make contact with the natural world, and sense or meaning need no longer be seen as the reference of signifiers to each other. Rather, the 'meaning' of a sign is a measure of the probability of triggering a particular material process.

In other words, signs do not merely represent or refer as though the semiotic occupies a non-material self-enclosed realm that must then somehow try to establish a connection with the material world. The semiotic includes the material. So signs can have material effects on other signs by initiating a process of assembling with the result that other signs are then ordered. Note that this is consequential in that a sign must be understood to not only have material effects, it also goes against a strict understanding of the autonomy of signs as constituting self-contained and sharply bounded systems. This, too, is why Deleuze and Guattari recognize the need for 'mixed semiotics', the idea that there are multiple

---

[3] The influence of complexity theory in linguistics itself is nothing new (Larsen-Freeman and Cameron 2008; Schmid 2020; Schneider 2020). What I want to emphasize here, however, is less complexity theory than the nature of assemblages. That is, the works in linguistics that draw on complexity theory tend to focus on conventional understandings of what counts as language (recognizable words and phrases) and present a view that is usage-based, dynamic and adaptive. The properties of words and phrases that make up a language are seen to result (correctly) from the communicative activities of users and the establishment of conventions of usage, as in, for example, Schmid's (2020) Entrenchment and Conventionalization Model. The assemblage focus, in contrast, takes the idea of what counts as conventional linguistic units themselves to be something that cannot be taken for granted. In this regard, whether fonts, translation apps, autocorrect functions or even users themselves should be considered part of the linguistic assemblage is open to question (see the discussion below on interiority and exteriority and also the discussion in section 5 on being 'linguistically curious').

regimes of signification that do not necessarily fall into neatly demarcated and consistently separable systems (Bonta and Protevi 2004: 8).

Deleuze and Guattari (1987: 174, 306) use the term 'deterritorialization' to describe the process by which elements of an extant assemblage dissemble and go on to form a new assemblage or 'reterritorialize'. They distinguish between 'relative deterritorialization' and 'absolute deterritorialization' (1987: 142, 510). In relative deterritorialization, the self-organization follows the patterns that have already been conventionalized whereas in absolute deterritorialization, the self-organization exhibits the system's 'capacity for self-transformation' (Bonta and Protevi 2004: 20).

The second thing to appreciate is that the constituent parts of any assemblage are themselves assemblages. There is no final point where we can be assured of having arrived at some elemental entity that has such a stable interior/exterior. In all likelihood, we have only arrived at yet another assemblage. Indeed, this is what makes Deleuze and Guattari's notion of an assemblage so radical (Haggerty and Ericson (2000: 608; emphasis added):

> Deleuze and Guattari introduce a radical notion of multiplicity into phenomena which we traditionally approach as being discretely bounded, structured and stable . . . *To dig beneath the surface stability of any entity is to encounter a host of different phenomena and processes working in concert.* The radical nature of this vision becomes more apparent when one realizes how any particular assemblage is itself composed of different discrete assemblages which are themselves multiple.

This radicalness arises from the realization that things that are typically assumed to have an internal unity and thus (by virtue of this unity) a built-in or naturally endowed boundary – such that this boundary serves to externally and 'naturally' distinguish one thing from some other – are, in fact, heterogeneously constituted internally. By extension, then, the boundaries that we otherwise often take for granted as unproblematically bestowing 'thingness' are themselves contingent.

The third thing to appreciate follows from the preceding point. Precisely because the component parts of an assemblage are always in the process of being assembled and reassembled, the relation between the parts is one of exteriority rather than interiority. A relation of interiority assumes that the 'component parts are constituted by the very relations they have to other parts in the whole' and 'a part detached from such a whole ceases to be what it is, since being this particular part is one of its constitutive properties' (DeLanda 2006: 9). Component parts derive their existence from being members of the whole, so that the latter is attributed an ontological significance greater than the former (as in structural functionalism).

In contrast, the concept of an assemblage demands that we instead acknowledge and give greater focus to relations of exteriority (DeLanda 2006: 10–11; emphasis in original):

> These relations imply, first of all, that a component part of an assemblage may be detached from it and plugged into a different assemblage in which its interactions are different.

Relations of exteriority make no assumptions about how changes to the component parts necessarily serve the larger totality, much less how they contribute to improving the latter's adaptive capacity. Rather, because the component parts bear only a contingent relationship to the totality and, indeed, to other component parts, any change observed vis-à-vis a component part may be maladaptive (where the totality is concerned) or may be motivated by factors that have little to do with adaptation.

Consider the example of a city. If we assume that a city's components are in a relation of interiority vis-à-vis one another, we are taking the view that these components (inhabitants, homes, schools, etc.) all form a neatly integrated whole, possibly designed to fit into an abstract sociological master plan along the lines of structural functionalism (Parsons 1960, 1971) or the Chicago School's view of the city as an adaptive organism. Such approaches fail 'to include as *constituent* elements of planning the conflict, ambiguity, and indeterminacy characteristic of social life' (Holston 1999: 46; emphasis in original).

It is worth emphasizing that 'interiority' does not mean 'internal' and neither does 'exteriority' mean 'external'. Both terms refer to the components of an entity. But they highlight the different ways in which the relations between the components can be understood. I have discussed the components of a city here, the point being that the components are in a relationship of exteriority to one another. That is, heterogeneous components are brought together in assembling a city. Even if we were to focus on a relationship of rivalry between two different cities, the understanding that we are looking at two separate cities is itself actually the result of deciding to *not* assemble the distinct units under the same rubric. But it could of course happen that erstwhile separate cities are understood as subparts of a larger single city, especially if socioeconomic and political forces decide that there are advantages to such a larger municipal assemblage. If this were to occur, then what was at one point two different cities would now be a single larger city. This combination of two cities into one, too, represents a relation of exteriority. Consider, for instance, the following description of Los Angeles, taken from a popular travel website (www.timeout.com/los-angeles/features/33/los-angeles-area-guide; accessed 25 January 2021):Precisely what constitutes Los Angeles is a matter for interpretation . . .

Los Angeles County contains 88 incorporated cities, each with its own juris-diction; among them are Santa Monica, Beverly Hills, Culver City, Pasadena and Los Angeles itself. To add to the confusion, some areas (for instance, East LA and Marina del Rey) are unincorporated, under the jurisdiction of Los Angeles County but not the city. While West Hollywood is an independent city, Hollywood is just one of many neighborhoods in the city of Los Angeles.

These points are encapsulated by Purcell (2002: 105; emphasis added), who points out that it is by no means at all clear or uncontroversial as to what actually constitutes the city:

> If the urban scale becomes the predominant scale that differentiates inside from outside, its parameters will have to be defined. The politics of scale literature makes clear that scales (such as the urban) are not pregiven or self-evident; rather they are socially produced through political struggle. Therefore, in order to define the geography of the political community that is bound together by the right to the city, and in order to define who is entitled to its rights and who is not, the urban scale will have to be defined through a process of struggle ... *For example, clearly 'Los Angeles' would involve more than just the municipal jurisdiction. The limits to the city would likely extend to the urbanized area of the city. But how extensive would these limits be? Would residents of Tijuana be considered residents of Los Angeles? According to what criteria?*

But the recursivity of assemblages and the relation of exteriority between the component parts mean that there is no final point at which the constituents of an assemblage, however careful and meticulous the planning, cohere seamlessly. New schools, homes and commercial districts may be added in manners that are to varying degrees unexpected and ad hoc. The influence of external elements such as climate change or a pandemic will force the components to adjust and adapt in locally differentiated ways. Needless to say, a relation of exteriority constitutes a more accurate and realistic understanding of how the parts of a city relate to another.

It should be clear that relations of exteriority follow from taking seriously the nature of assemblages. This is because if assemblages are themselves the results of bringing together a heterogeneous collection of objects, then we have no grounds for assuming that this collection of objects should fit each other in any a priori manner such that their relation to the resulting assemblage is one of interiority.

I now turn to the implications of assemblages for our understanding of language.

2.6 The Linguistic Assemblage

2.6.1 Regularities in Language

We know that there are regularities in language, even if these regularities are not without exceptions. The marking of number (English) or gender (Italian), for example, follows fairly clear and specifiable patterns or rules. But there are also particular lexical items that are exceptions to the rules, either existing as isolated examples or constituting sub-regularities within the wider morphological patterns.

This is a point that even extends to longer grammatical constructions, such as the covariational conditional *The Xer the Yer* (e.g. The more you think about it, the less you understand), the ditransitive *Subj V Obj1 Obj2* (e.g. He baked her a muffin) (Goldberg 2005: 5) and the *What's X doing Y?* construction (Kay and Fillmore 1999). The last is a relatively idiomatic construction exemplified by expressions such as 'What's this fly doing in my soup?' and 'What is this scratch doing on the table?'. 'What's' and 'doing' are lexically invariant parts of the construction while 'X' and 'Y' represent open slots that can be satisfied by various noun phrases. The construction has a very specific pragmatics associated with it. It does not simply ask about an activity; rather, it indicates the speaker's judgment that there is an incongruity, such as the presence of the fly in the soup.

When speakers use these constructions, the conventionalized linguistic properties constrain the usage so that there is usually a shared understanding as to what parts of a construction are open and what parts are not. But this shared understanding is neither stable nor can it be taken for granted. Speakers make their own inferences as to which parts of a construction are more malleable and which parts are not. As a result, even speakers with the 'same community' can have slightly differing ideas about the pragmatic and lexicogrammatical properties of a construction (Hoffmann and Trousdale 2013).

The important point to appreciate is this: speakers assemble language in ways that reflect their own encounters with and understandings of particular constructions. Even shared understandings of constructions are contingent on speakers' interpretations of these constructions. Such interpretations may change over time, leading to divergent understandings as well. There is no condition under which speakers can be said to ever encounter a language system or variety in its totality; encounters are only ever with constructions. This brings us to the next point.

2.6.2 There Is No Language in its Totality

All our experiences with language are only via particular material signs. More precisely, all our experiences with language are via particular signs that we learn to categorize as 'linguistic' in contrast to 'non-linguistic' and, within the former, as belonging to, say, 'English' or 'Japanese' or 'bad English' or 'standard English' etc. This observation speaks to a simple truth that the concept of an assemblage brings out very clearly: the system or variety that the particular signs belong to is *assembled*.

We encounter signs that we learn as part of our socialization into the speech practices and language ideologies of the communities that we are part of and we learn to assemble these signs by categorizing them as belonging to 'English' or 'Malay', as the case may be. Language as an autonomous system or variety is never apprehended in its totality. The notion of language in its totality is a complete misunderstanding of the nature of language. It is a post hoc notion that we have bought into only because we started off wrongly with the assumption of an autonomous system or variety and the totality that such an assumption implies, as well as the relations of interiority that are presumed to characterize the parts of such systems/varieties. But qua assemblage, language is an ongoing project, with different bits added and others removed at various times. And since we can never encounter the complete collection of signs that might be said to constitute the system or variety in toto, any attempt to argue for the reality any such system or variety is really the result of an extrapolation fallacy: an unwarranted move from the particular collection of signs actually encountered to the postulation of a complete and autonomous system that the collection supposedly adumbrates.

Thinking in terms of assemblages avoids the extrapolation fallacy for the simple reason that it is not committed to any kind of talk of a linguistic system or variety beyond the collection of signs that are otherwise taken as indicating the existence of the former. It is the collection itself that constitutes the assemblage, not anything beyond that. And as the components of the collection change, so too does the assemblage. From this fundamentally important observation comes a simple corollary. There is absolutely no reason why we should all share exactly the same understanding of the linguistic assemblage, be this 'English' or 'Malay' or something else, since different individuals likely to have different collections of signs in mind and the same individual may even have different collections of signs in mind at different times. There will likely be overlaps across these different collections of signs and often these overlaps are sufficient that the differences in understanding what constitutes the assemblage don't matter. But there is no escaping the fact of the matter that the differences are also present and any theory about of language has to be able to account for both the differences as well as the similarities.

Thus, consider that there are different ways of assembling English in Thailand. There are websites that seem to assume that the existence of 'Tinglish' or 'Thaiglish' can be taken for granted, as shown by the following examples.

(i) The site, www.into-asia.com (accessed 31 January 2015) describes 'Tinglish' as the 'Thai version of English' where sentences 'are simplistic but still easily understandable':

For instance, 'I didn't want to go yesterday' would likely be said instead as 'Yesterday I not want go'. There's also the doubling of a few English words where it happens in Thai e.g. 'same same', 'near near' etc.

(ii) Stewart (2013) states that 'Tinglish' 'can also be know [sic] as Thaiglish', and is 'the non-standard form (on) English used by native Thai speakers due to language interference'.

(iii) www.theknowledge.in.th (accessed 31 January 2015) asks rhetorically:

Ever heard of the word *Tinglish* or *Thaiglish*? They are the unofficial terms used to describe the fusion of the Thai language with the English language often producing a new word with a meaning that may or may not be grammatically correct ... When a Thai person says that '*These pants are fit* what they really do mean is that '*These pants are too small*'. *Fit* is Thaiglish for *small*.

(iv) Lee and Nadeau (2011: 1123) suggest that:

Tenglish (pronounced 'tinglish') is characterized as the English spoken by Thais, while Englithai refers to the Thai spoken by Anglophones or native English speakers. The third form, Thaiglish, is characterized as a bona fide hybrid language, which conflates the Thai and English language structure and vocabulary ...
Tenglish is merely an adaptation of English and will generally lack particles, articles and/or correct grammar conjugation ...
Thai Americans will often try to speak in the Thaiglish form, which adapts the Thai language rhythm, tone, and pattern. Thaiglish speakers will retain Thai pronunciation, tonality, and question tags like 'na' and 'ja' and particles like 'krub' and 'ka' to soften their tone, indicate respect, a request, encouragement or other moods ... Another characteristic of Thaiglish is adding suffixs [sic] like '-ing' when words cannot be directly translated or clearly described in one English word. For example, the term 'wai-ing' as in 'I am wai-ing my aunt' is often used amongst Thai Americans when one is referring to the traditional Thai form of greeting someone.

Whereas the definition of 'Tinglish' in (i) focuses on linguistic features, those provided in (ii) and (iii) tie language use to the identity of its speakers. These are clearly different ways of constituting the linguistic assemblage referred to as 'Tinglish/Thaiglish'. (iv) also links the identification of a variety to speaker identity, making further distinctions between Thai Americans, (regular) Thais and Anglophones. The point here, of course, is not that one definition should be given greater weight than another. Rather, from an assemblage perspective, such multiple and at times conflicting understandings of Englithai, Tenglish and Thaiglish are to be expected.

2.6.3 Circulation Involves Assembling and Reassembling

Thinking of language as an assemblage also carries important implications for how we conceptualize the spread or circulation of a language. We tend to think of circulation as one way in which a language becomes common/shared. However, there is a tension between talking about a language being shared, on the one hand, and acknowledging that it circulates, on the other hand. As Blommaert (2010) points out in his discussion of language as a mobile resource, mobility creates unpredictability because language gets dislodged from its traditional settings; and its traditional functions become distorted by the processes of mobility as language gets inserted into new settings (2010: 197). This process of insertion changes – in ways that are both subtle and not so subtle – both the new settings as well as the language itself.

We have seen that the circulation of English (as in the case of English in Thailand) does not only lead to the emergence of different named varieties but different ways of constituting the linguistic assemblage. This testifies to the distortion/fragmentation that results from the circulation of a language. If this is so, then it becomes pertinent to inquire further into the relationship between circulation and sharing. Does the circulation of a language and the distortions that may result mean that it is not at all possible to talk about the language being shared? And if a language can indeed be shared, then what are we to make of the distortions entailed by its circulation?

The circulation of language necessarily results in a wider and more diverse range of interactions. Concomitantly, the perceived unity of a language – as encapsulated in the name given to that language, such as 'Thaiglish' – is really an abstraction over many different linguistic constructions of varying sizes (word, phrase, entire sentence-level constructions) that can also be regular to varying degrees.

We also know that one of the key controversies regarding the circulation of English is the question of whether the so-called new or nativized varieties[4] should be treated as legitimate varieties in their own right or whether they should be seen as deficient versions of more established varieties. The broad characterization of these controversies, from the perspective of Kachru's Three Circles Model, its theoretical problems notwithstanding (Park and Wee 2012), is that the Inner Circle varieties are considered to be established Englishes whose legitimacy is assured. Outer Circle varieties tend to be viewed even by their own speakers with a degree of insecurity and schizophrenia, where a sense of these varieties ought to be granted their own legitimacy sits uneasily with the

---

[4] It should be clear that 'varieties' here refers to a collection of constructions rather than some linguistic totality.

worry that they are still not quite as good enough as their Inner Circle counter-parts. Finally, in the Expanding Circle, questions of legitimacy are less of a concern because of a strong sense of exonormativity, where it is taken for granted that speakers should indeed be looking to the more established varieties as references for what would be considered good/standard English.

To the extent, then, that attitudes towards a variety are strongly exonorma-tive, we have once again a case of what Deleuze and Guattari term relative deterritorialization (now on a macro scale). That is, exonormativity means that any calibration of variety's linguistic practices will tend to be done with a more established or more prestigious variety in mind, thus following (albeit imperfectly) the more established linguistic conventions and templates asso-ciated with that latter variety. In contrast, to the extent that the attitudes are strongly endonormative, where there is a desire to establish the newly emer-ging variety as having its own linguistic identity and legitimacy independent of a more established variety, then we have a case of absolute deterritorialization.

The notions of relative and absolute deterritorialization give us concrete ways of understanding just what it means for a sign to be material and to be able to trigger a process of self-organization. In particular, metalinguistic signs such as 'English' or 'Malay' or 'Singlish' have material effects because they trigger the calibration of linguistic practices that are aimed at – to varying degrees and depending on the specific social and political issues at hand – either further accentuating or downplaying the differences between one var-iety and another.

In this way, metalinguistic signs do not merely refer to or represent a particular linguistic entity; they can also serve as rallying points around which the linguistic practices of entire groups of speakers coalesce. As I point out elsewhere (Wee 2018b), it doesn't matter if the variety that the metalinguistic sign names is only emerging or already well-established since: 'The very fact that a specific variety's name is being bandied about in public discourse indicates that there are publicly contested ideologies regarding language at work.' Metalinguistic signs help to calibrate linguistic practices; they are signs that affect both the regimes of linguistic signs as well as the actions of speakers. And this, of course, returns us to the point that the linguistic system cannot be treated as autonomous or self-contained. Rather, we are looking at a case of 'mixed semiotics'.

2.6.4 Decentring, Re-Centring and Reconceptualizing Language

The concept of an assemblage – by drawing attention to the importance and relevance of 'mixed semiotics' – encourages us to further examine prevailing assumptions about the ontology of language. Why, for example, should we limit the material dimension to words (whether spoken or written)? On what grounds do we exclude the speakers/writers or the mode of communication (phone, book, blog)? Consider what we understand by graffiti. It is 'outlawed literacy' or 'criminalized' (Conquergood 1997: 354–5) precisely because its appearance on public surfaces is 'deemed a threat to property, propriety and pristine walls' (Pennycook (2008: 137). Once abstracted away from the public surface on which words and pictures may have been illegally painted, the language used no longer constitutes graffiti. Likewise, the different ways of assembling English in Thailand (see above) also require acknowledgement of the materiality of language.

We have to consistently understand the linguistic assemblage as the product of activity, human and non-human. And changes to language – including what we may each differentially take to be language – are the results of changing activities. For example, in a BBC travel show, an English speaker travelled across China using a translation app on his mobile phone to communicate with the locals. His English utterances were translated by the app, with varying degrees of communicative success into Mandarin, which would then play the translated version for his Chinese interlocutors. In this regard, we have to seriously consider that the Mandarin 'spoken' by the app on the phone is not the same Mandarin as that spoken among the Chinese. The differences in some instances may be negligible; yet, in other cases, the apparently nonsensical output leads to laughter from the interlocutors. We also have to consider that the English-speaking traveller is a kind of Mandarin 'speaker' when using the app, so that the app becomes an (occasional) extension of the speaker, a hybrid entity that we might characterize as a linguistic cyborg.

But what is more pertinent to the point being made here is that these different ways in which language, technology and humans combine should not be conceptualized as ways in which there is a linguistic constant, a uniform and invariant way in which language exists, one that floats above and is defined separately from these manifestations. To argue for such a conceptual linguistic constant is to simply presume that there is a metaphysically invariant and ontologically real phenomenon called 'language' apart from its materiality.

But the implication of assemblage theory is that there is no such linguistic constant. Different realizations of language, that is, varying combinations of humans, technology and what we might conventionally call 'language', are inescapably different ways of assembling language. There are no grounds for positing anything like a conceptual linguistic constant above and beyond the varied and multiple contingent assemblages.

2.7 Conclusion

Given what I have just said about the importance of decentring language and recognizing its materiality, any talk of a linguistic assemblage has to be really understood as a matter of relative descriptive emphasis. Language is being highlighted or foregrounded when reference is made to a linguistic assemblage. But there should be no assumption that non-linguistic modalities are being excluded or that language is in any way necessarily more important than these other modalities or that it is even stable as to what ought to count as language.

These ideas, as the next two sections will show, carry important implications for the study of world Englishes.

3 Creativity and World Englishes

3.1 Introduction

In this section, I consider the issue of creativity in world Englishes. In response to an earlier intervention by Kachru (1995), which looks at what he calls 'literary creativity', Widdowson (2019) argues for the importance of recognizing 'the creativity of common talk'. We will see that the discussions by Kachru and Widdowson of these two types of creativity critically depend on accepting that language use can be linked to distinct communities and their associated varieties of English – in this case, the distinction involves the three Kachruvian Circles: Inner, Outer and Expanding.

In what follows, I first summarize the contributions from Kachru and Widdowson. I then highlight the problems involved before demonstrating what an account from a posthumanist perspective would look like. I show, via an analysis of two YouTube videos, that if we are prepared to recognize assemblages, we can arrive at a more nuanced appreciation of creativity in world Englishes.

3.2 Creativity Encircled

In his earlier discussion, Kachru (1995) calls for the recognition of the 'literary creativity' of English from writers from the Outer Circle. The Outer Circle, in Kachru's Three Circles Model, refers to those countries (e.g. Malaysia, Singapore, the Philippines) in which English had taken root as a result of the historical processes of colonization and, more recently, institutionalization and where, as a consequence, nativized varieties have developed.

Kachru's decision to focus on the Outer Circle stems from the fact that there was apparently little doubt that writers from the Inner Circle, that is, those countries in which English 'originated' (e.g. Britain, the USA) are fully capable of using English creatively for literary purposes. But there remained at the time of Kachru's writing (and still remains to some extent to this day) questions, uncertainties and insecurities as to whether writers who are located outside the Inner Circle can also be legitimately described as being capable of literary creativity using English.

Kachru is specifically concerned with legitimizing the works of writers in the Outer Circle who are trying to appropriate English as a vehicle for expressing their own cultural perspectives. Kachru's (1997) argument for literary creativity deals with what he calls 'transcultural creativity' in 'English-using speech communities'. He asserts that (1997: 70):

> In discussions of literary creativity, there is still a generally held – though erroneous – view that the 'mother tongue' is the primary medium of literary creativity across cultures and that creativity in the other tongue is a deviation from the norm ... The multilingual's use of English in various literary contexts in world Englishes provides abundant data for transcultural creativity.

Kachru is arguing here against the assumption that literary creativity is only possible if one uses one's mother tongue. In the case of a person from the Outer Circle, the mother tongue is presumably not English and, hence, any attempt to use of English for creative purposes would run the risk of being deemed ill-conceived and illegitimate. Kachru is instead suggesting that such attempts to appropriate English should be treated as illustrations of 'transcultural creativity', where the individual, presumably multilingual in his or her own mother tongue as well as the 'other tongue', English, is choosing the latter as the medium of creative expression. Kirkpatrick (2014: 39) provides 'two examples of African writers capturing the nuances and rhetorical tropes of local languages while writing in English':

> The first passage is from the novel The Voice by the Nigerian novelist Gabriel Okara, and is taken from Bokamba (1982) ... Here the local use of repetition in Nigerian languages for emphasis and effect is evident, as is a distinctive use of word order. The second example comes from the novel, Sozaboy: A Novel in Rotten English, written by the Nigerian activist Ken Saro-Wiwa, and published in 1985 (Saro-Wiwa 1985) ... Again, the use of repetition is evident, as is the use of a discourse marker, 'na', borrowed from the local Ogoni languages.

Note that very little is said about literary creativity in the Expanding Circles: those countries (such as China, Japan, Thailand) in which English is still considered a foreign language. This is a problematic gap that we will return to below.

Widdowson (2019: 312) accepts Kachru's argument that it is not valid to assume 'that literary creativity is something within the exclusive privileged preserve of Inner Circle native speakers' and acknowledges that Kachru does 'give a convincing demonstration of how literary writers from the Outer Circle have their own distinctive ways of making creative use of the language which are uniquely expressive of the cultural values of their own communities'. However, Widdowson wants to also draw attention to the fact that creativity is not limited to literary uses. In this regard, he chooses to focus on English use in the Expanding Circles.

Interestingly, Widdowson, too, skirts the question of literary creativity in the Expanding Circles. Situating his arguments within the English as a lingua franca (ELF) enterprise (Jenkins 2007; Seidlhofer 2011), Widdowson (2019: 317; emphasis added) argues that 'What we typically find in ELF communication is the *creativity of common talk*' and he (2019: 314) suggests that 'a message can be said to be creative when it conforms to encoding principles without conforming to usage conventions'. Examples, according to Widdowson, might include 'advices' and 'evidences' as the unconventional pluralization of mass nouns. In ELF communication, then, 'though the language produced . . . may be abnormal as usage, it can serve the entirely normal function of pragmatic use' (Widdowson 2019: 316).[5]

To summarize, the debate about creativity in world Englishes has tended to focus on the use of English in the Outer and Expanding Circles and, with this focus, a distinction made between literary creativity and creativity in common talk. The former is credited to the Outer Circle and the latter to the Expanding Circle. However, there is little said about the converse, that is, whether the Outer Circle deserves to be also credited with creativity in common talk and whether the Expanding Circle can, too, be said to possess literary creativity.

There are a number of curious features about the way this debate has been framed. For one, the issue of creativity in English is not at all in question where the Inner Circle is concerned. Creativity in English in the Inner Circle is taken for granted and there appears to be no need to excavate the matter. As a consequence, discussions about whether the distinction between literary and common talk creativity is also pertinent to the Inner Circle or whether the distinction is neutralized do not arise. If the former is the case, that is, if the distinction also applies to the Inner Circle, then we need to grapple with further questions such as these: Exactly how is the distinction between 'literary' and

---

[5] There are severe conceptual problems with the entire ELF enterprise. And by situating his arguments within the ELF enterprise, Widdowson unfortunately inherits those problems. I will not repeat those arguments here. Interested readers can refer to Maley (2010), Park and Wee (2011) and Prodromou (2008), among others.

'common talk' to be preserved? Is it by genre? By speaker's illocutionary intent? By perlocutionary effect? If it is the last that is the case, that is, if the distinction is neutralized, then even more difficult questions surface: What are the socio-political-cultural-linguistic factors that would allow for such a neutralization? And would it be possible that the Outer and Expanding Circles might also, in due course, come to enjoy such a neutralization?

As things stand, it seems that it is only within the Outer and Expanding Circles that the issue of creativity (whether it is at all possible and, if so, what kind) arises. We see this issue recurring in Widdowson's assertion that ELF creativity (Pitzl 2018) is somehow different or special. But what Widdowson describes as 'creativity in common talk' in the Expanding Circle has in actuality long been noted even in the so-called Inner Circle Englishes. The point to appreciate, of course, is that common talk creativity is not a special or noteworthy feature of any Circle. For example, Fillmore, Kay and O'Connor (1988) draw most of their examples from American English and they note that the grammar of a language displays varying degrees of idiomaticity. There are constructional instances of 'unfamiliar pieces familiarly arranged', such as *kith and kin* (1988: 506) as well as 'familiar pieces unfamiliarly arranged', such as *all of a sudden* (1988: 508). The pluralization of mass nouns such as advices' and 'evidences' – the result of what Widdowson calls 'conforming to encoding principles' – is clearly a case of 'familiar pieces unfamiliarly arranged'. It is the result of analogizing mass nouns along the behavioural lines of count nouns and analogy has long been recognized as a mechanism for grammatical change and development (Hopper and Traugott 1993).

Two, the debate over creativity vis-à-vis the Outer and Expanding Circles is about creativity 'in' English. The focus is on English as a medium for the expression of human creativity and with that, an undertheorized understanding of agency. Little to no attention is given to the contributory role that tools – including language itself – might play in the actualization of creativity. Along such lines, what is being contested is whether the language itself (in this case, English) can be appropriated by speakers for whom it is not the mother tongue to convey their particular cultural values and perspectives. And while this appropriation certainly involves making changes to English (i.e. 'nativization'), the language itself is treated as an inert albeit malleable medium, a flexible tool that serves the expression of human creativity. We see this in Kachru's (1997: 70) statement above, as well as in Kirkpatrick's description of the African examples. This is also the case with Widdowson's discussion of the pluralization of mass nouns as supposedly illustrative of the unique creativity of ELF common talk.

All of this comes as no surprise, of course, given the anthropocentricism in language studies. But there are problems with downplaying the role of tools, including language, as mere instruments of human agency. This becomes clear when we consider the matter of indexicality.

3.3 Indexicality[6]

Indexicality (Eckert 2008; Silverstein 2003) highlights the fact that the meanings of linguistic features are tied to specific contexts of usage. Indexicality is closely linked to style (including non-linguistic style systems relating to dress, location, among others) and influenced by ideologies pertaining to language but also to other ideologies that are more broadly social, political and cultural in nature (such as commodification, identity, neoliberalism, to name just a few).

As a consequence, once a linguistic (or non-linguistic, for that matter) feature becomes highlighted as a potential resource (or liability), that very act of highlighting itself can 'change the meaning both of the resource and of the original style, hence changing the semiotic landscape' (Eckert 2008: 457). All these considerations point to the properties of linguistic features being open-ended and ever changing.

For example, Eckert (2012) discusses Labov's (1963) study of how the diphthong /ay/, marks the speaker as coming from Martha's Vineyard. This would constitute a first-order indexical (Silverstein 2003). But while some Vineyarders had been lowering the nucleus of the diphthong so as to converge more closely to the pronunciation of the mainlanders, others reversed this pronunciation trend so as to avoid a lowering of the nucleus. This would constitute a second-order indexical, where the speaker is not just projecting her identity as a Vineyarder but as a specific kind of Vineyarder, as someone who is arguably more authentic than those other Vineyarders whose pronunciation more closely resembles that of the mainlanders (Eckert 2012: 88). And, of course, there is no reason why the indexical order should stop only at two so that multiple indexical orders are not only possible but typical.

This growth in indexical orders leads Eckert (2008) to introduce the notion of an indexical field so as to highlight that a linguistic feature can be associated with 'a constellation of ideologically linked meanings, any region of which can be invoked in context' (Eckert 2012: 94). As an example, Campbell-Kibler (2007) shows that the velar variant (as in 'talking') tends to be associated with intelligence, formality and sophistication whereas the non-velar version (as in 'talkin'') tends to be associated with the absence of these attributes. Another example comes from Eckert (2008: 469), who notes that the indexical field of /t/

---

[6] The discussion in this section draws on Wee (2018: 256ff).

release can include meanings such as 'being a school teacher', 'being British', 'being formal', 'being emphatic', 'being exasperated', 'being educated', 'being elegant' and 'being a gay diva'. Some of these are social types ('British', 'school teacher', 'gay diva'), others are relatively stable attributes ('educated', 'articulate'), while yet others are stances that can change quite quickly and easily ('exasperated', 'emphatic').

Importantly, these categories should not be taken as representing hard distinctions within the indexical field. Rather, the relations between them are highly fluid (Eckert 2008: 469), which is why it is useful to speak on an indexical potential (Eckert 2012: 97), where in any instance of the feature being used, a number of the categories could be activated rather than just a single determinate category. And speakers may not always have a clear or determinate sense of which specific category/categories is/are being 'activated' by the use of the feature. In this way, 'indexicality is one of the points where the social and cultural order enters language and communicative behavior' (Blommaert 2005: 172).

The phenomenon of indexicality is a clear demonstration of the importance of adopting a posthumanist perspective. While indexicality is an interpretation of signs,[7] the interpretation itself is not fully 'free'. It is always constrained by what the signs already bring with them as parts of their meanings. Each speaker thus encounters the (linguistic) sign as already imbued with conceptual content and interprets/utilizes that sign based on his/her understanding of that content. In this way, signs possess what Bennett (2010: 20) has dubbed 'thing-power'. Although she acknowledges the unwieldiness of the term, her use of the term 'thing-power' is intended to capture the fact that 'a lot happens to the concept of agency once nonhuman things are figured less as social construction and more as actors, and once humans themselves are assessed not as autonoms but as vital materialities' (2010: 21).

Speakers therefore do not simply wield or use language as though the latter were 'instruments of human volition' (Hazard 2013: 66), as inert material that can be freely modified or changed. Language comes with its own contributory properties. Admittedly, these are properties that owe their existence to human activities. But then, so are guns (see section 1). And recall that the point of posthumanism has never been to deny the role of human agency. Rather it has been to give the agentive properties of non-human actors their due. The fact of indexicality is a good reminder that signs are further interpretable only because they are to some extent already prepacked with meaning. Indexicality *ex nihilo*

---

[7] Let us agree that the ability to interpret signs requires conscious awareness so that humans and other animals can interpret signs. It is not clear, at least as things stand technologically, that machines are capable of interpreting signs.

is a nonstarter and, by implication, so is creativity (of whatever stripe) involving language.

With this in mind, we can now turn to two examples that challenge the accounts of creativity in world Englishes from Kachru and Widdowson.

3.4 Creativity Assembled

Example 1: 'Taehyung saying "I purple you" – a compilation'[8] (www .youtube.com/watch?v=2TZv6hcKI_U; accessed 17 July 2020)
Consider the use of 'purple' as a verb, as in 'I purple you'. This specific usage has been credited to Kim Tae Hyung, also known as V, a member of the globally successful K-Pop group BTS, who says it means that 'I will trust and love you for a long time' (www.urbandictionary.com/define.php?term=I%20Purple% 20You; accessed 18 July 2020; www.newsweek.com/bts-kim-taehyung-purple-meaning-1453501; accessed 18 July 2020).

The group has a fanbase known as ARMY. The verb 'purple' in this context is therefore used mainly by BTS to express its appreciation to ARMY, by ARMY to express its devotion to BTS and by individual fans to signal their shared membership in ARMY. In these contexts, it is not uncommon for the phrase 'I/We Purple You' to be accompanied by a purple heart emoji or even for the emoji itself to completely replace the verb. Here are some examples:

(i) I Purple You
(ii) I purple you BTS
(iii) I will purple you forever
(iv) We are Purpling each other
(v) I ♥ you
(vi) ♥ ♥♥

There are a number of observations worth making regarding this use of 'purple'. One, it problematizes the distinction between literary and common talk creativity. It is undoubtedly 'creative' in that Kim Tae Hyung explicitly decided to give a new meaning and new syntactic category to the colour (www .cheatsheet.com/entertainment/bts-fans-celebrate-the-anniversary-of-i-purple-you.html/; accessed 19 July 2020):At BTS's 3rd Muster in November 2016, V coined the phrase 'I purple you.'

> 'Do you know what purple means?' He asked the audience. 'Purple is the last colour of the rainbow colours. Purple means I will trust and love you for a long time. I just made it up.' . . . 'I wish I could see you for a long time just

---
[8] The discussion of K-Pop and K-Drama has benefitted enormously from insights provided by Nora Samosir. All errors that remain are my own.

like the meaning of purple', he said. 'We will always trust you and go up the stairs with you. You don't need to help us all the time. You can hold our hands and follow us now. We'll go up really high. I'll make it nice.' . . .

Fans also thanked V for creating the phrase about the special connection BTS and ARMY share. 'I don't know how much we have to thank to Taehyung for making this lovely and fresh expression. It's been 3 years since our genius, Taehyung made "I Purple you" He literally invented a new meaning and culture of purple colour', one fan wrote on Twitter.

Here is a case of changing indexicalities. V first describes 'purple' not simply as a colour but links it to its position as the last colour of the rainbow. The reference to the rainbow primes the audience to associate 'purple' with something positive, which is confirmed when V explains that he wants 'purple', as a verb, to express unwavering affection, devotion, loyalty and support. He furthermore explicitly states that the change in 'purple' is something that 'I just made it up myself'. So, this would seem to be a case of literary creativity. But it is also common talk creativity in that 'purple' is used as part of the way in which BTS and ARMY communicate. It is a marker of in-group identity, used by fans to signal their shared membership in ARMY and to distinguish themselves from those who are not ARMY. 'Purple' thus also presents us with second-order indexicality.

Two, this group comprising BTS and ARMY is a very large group indeed. While arriving at an exact figure is close to impossible, one estimate is that there were '48 million unique authors mentioning BTS online' between 2013 and 2019 (www.brandwatch.com/blog/bts-facts-and-statistics/#:~:text=The% 20BTS%20fans%20call%20themselves,between%20400%2C000%20and% 201%2C000%2C000%20soldiers; accessed 18 July 2020). So, even though we are looking at just one lexicogrammatical construction (albeit with variants), it is a construction with very wide usage. This leads to the next point.

Three, BTS is one of the most successful acts globally. The music of BTS has hit the number one spot in USA, UK, Australia, Canada etc. It has been estimated that 'BTS' contribution to South Korea's GDP is almost comparable with Korean Air' (https://medium.com/@shadow_twts/the-bts-effect-on-south -koreas-economy-industry-and-culture-975e8933da56; accessed 18 July 2020). Their last three concerts in 2019 raked in a total of US$860.7 million (www .koreaherald.com/view.php?ud=20191223000424#:~:text=K%2Dpop%20boy %20band%20BTS,an%20academic%20report%20showed%20Monday. &text=The%20team%20estimated%20that%20some,of%20them%20attend ing%20the%20concerts; accessed 18 July 2020). Moreover, BTS is a key contributor to South Korea's tourism (ibid):

The number of BTS-driven foreign tourists accounts for about 67 per cent of some 280,000 foreign tourists who visited South Korea during the run of the

2018 PyeongChang Winter Olympics the country hosted, the report also showed.

The report also stressed unquantifiable economic effect of the BTS concert. Having developed interest in Korean culture and the Korean language thanks to BTS, its fans had a wish to study or work in the band's home country, an effect, the team pointed out, of bringing in foreign human capital.

Thus, the lexicogrammatical construction is not necessarily just a South Korean phenomenon if by this we mean that its use is restricted to South Korea or South Koreans. Apparently, the top ten countries with the most BTS fans (in descending order) are: the Philippines, South Korea, Thailand, Vietnam, Indonesia, Malaysia, Brazil, USA, Taiwan and Mexico (www.kpopmap.com/the-countries -with-the-most-bts-fans-in-the-world-are/; accessed 19 July 2020).

Fourth, the BTS example is just one part of the Hallyu wave or 'Korean Wave'. The term refers to the growth and global popularity of Korean culture and popular culture encompassing everything from music, movies, drama to online games and Korean cuisine just to name a few (https://martinroll.com /resources/articles/asia/korean-wave-hallyu-the-rise-of-koreas-cultural-economy-pop-culture/; accessed 19 July 2020). While an in-depth sociolinguistic study of Hallyu remains to be conducted, it has been noted that there are a number of words and phrases that tend to be associated with the phenomenon (http://hellotohallyu.com/home/k-pop-term-glossary/; accessed 19 July 2020; www.davidpublisher.org/Public/uploads/Contribute/5a740a29c5a9c.pdf; accessed 19 July 2020). Examples are shown below:

(2)

(i) The visual of the group (where 'the visual' refers to the most attractive member of a K-Pop group)

(ii) A: I have a job interview tomorrow.

B: Fighting! (Used as an exhortative to provide support or encouragement.)

(iii) Noona killer ('noona' is the Korean term meaning 'elder sister', used affectionately even when there is no biological relation. 'Noona killer' is a younger male who has a reputation for charming older females or *noonas*.)

Regardless of whether we are considering just 'purple' or the other examples in (2) as well, it would be questionable to suggest that we are looking at a variety of English (in Kachru's sense of an institutionalized and nativized version of English). It is not even clear that these uses of English constitute a register or that the users are using English as a lingua franca in Widdowson's sense of the term, where speakers depart from conventionalized usage without being aware that they are actually doing so and are thus not intending to 'draw attention to their non-conformities' (Widdowson 2019: 315). Nevertheless, any attempt to study the global spread of English should be able to say something about examples such as these.

The notion of an assemblage can provide a reasonable and coherent account of such creativity. Recall that one of the key points of a linguistic assemblage is that there is no language in its totality. Whether we want to focus on just 'purple' or 'purple' in conjunction with the various examples in (2), we are still looking at linguistic assemblages. Any talk of 'BTS English' or 'Hallyu English' or even just 'the BTS Purple Construction' draws on the notion of an assemblage.

And just as language in society does not exist in isolation but is rather also part of a multidimensional collectivity, so, too, does any focus on the linguistic assemblage simply represent the analyst's decision to focus on conventionally recognizable language such as 'purple'. The idea of a linguistic assemblage merely foregrounds the conventionally linguistic but there is no reason to treat the linguistic as having properties that intrinsically separate it from the non-linguistic (such as the use of the purple heart emoji). The relation between the (linguistic and non-linguistic) parts of the assemblage is one of exteriority rather than interiority. Creativity in the case of BTS's use of 'purple' is not purely linguistic. Rather, it involves drawing on the celebrity or symbolic capital that the group enjoys, being able to use that to impose a new meaning and syntax on 'purple' and to convert that new usage into further multimodal variants that then get used by ARMY as in-group solidarity markers. This is a small but neat example of how the circulation of language involves acts of assembling and reassembling, as the six variants in (1) demonstrate. Depending on whether we are interested in focusing just on 'BTS English' or 'Hallyu English' or even (nascent) 'Konglish/Korean English', we are at each analytical moment always giving attention to different assemblages.

We thus have to confront the question of what constitutes language itself. Is the purple heart emoji to be treated as part of 'Korean/BTS English' or language more generally given the widespread use of emojis in communication (Seargeant 2019)? Or should emojis be considered paralinguistic? Recall that the emoji can stand in for the verb 'purple' (see 1v). It should be noted that classifying emojis as 'paralinguistic' avoids the question of whether these are linguistic by merely asserting that they are not. In this regard, Wittgenstein's remarks about whether a language is ever complete are highly pertinent (1958: 8; emphasis added):

> [A]sk yourself whether our language is complete – *whether it was so before the symbolism of chemistry and the notation of the infinitesimal calculus were incorporated in it*; for these are, so to speak, suburbs of our language. (And how many houses or streets does it take before a town begins to be a town?) Our language can be seen as an ancient city: a maze of little streets and

squares, of old and new houses, and of houses with additions from various periods; and this surrounded by a multitude of new boroughs with straight regular streets and uniform houses.

The question of language completeness (and thus the distinction between the linguistic and the non-linguistic) does not apply only to emojis. It also applies to mathematical and chemical symbols. And it applies likewise to the use of hashtags. Examples of hashtagged phrases include Urban Outfitter's '#UOPRIDE' and Wells Fargo Bank's "#TOGETHERisBEAUTIFUL', both used in support of San Francisco's Gay Pride movement. A hashtag is a metadata tag that is used in social media. Its purpose is to allow users to find the collection of messages that have been posted using that hash.

Here, then, is a good demonstration of the materiality of language at work, where what is linguistically relevant is not just the phrase per se, but also the fact that it is being prefixed by a hash and thus the technological affordances and online intertextual opportunities that follow from being hashtagged. Crucially, whether we want to treat mathematical and chemical symbols, emojis or hashes as linguistic or non-linguistic is itself ultimately a matter of how we decide to define the linguistic assemblage. There is no prior non-assemblage basis on which any such decision or definition can be made.

Finally, note that such acts of assembling and reassembling would not have been possible without the contributing roles of YouTube as a platform on which videos can be presented and where comments can be shared, as well as fan blogs where enthusiasm for BTS and multiple uses of 'purple' can be further cele-brated across the globe. These technological affordances (Gibson 1966, 1979) cannot be dismissed as mere aids to the agency of human actors like BTS and ARMY. They are important agentive parts of the linguistic/K-Pop assemblage, possessing 'thing-power', without which the spread of particular linguistic usages would have been severely curtailed if not altogether impossible. There is here a 'volatile mix' (Bennett 2010) of emotions, human and non-human actors – all of which contribute, even if there is 'some friction among the parts', towards the intensity of K-Pop/Hallyu fandom.

Example 2: 'Sinful English' (www.youtube.com/watch?v=fiYXiixlV0A; accessed 20 May 2020)

Consider now another example. The 'Sinful English' video, available on YouTube, is a humorous guide on 'How to speak Singlish'. The video was produced by two US-based Singaporeans, Shawn Tan and Leandro Siow, and has been since been viewed at least 200,000 times since it was first uploaded (Rashith 2012). In the video, Americans are shown having 'first-world commu-nication problems' because proper English is too lengthy. Singlish is then presented as a remedy that allows for more effective and quick communication. Tan (Rashith 2012, no page numbers) states that 'Singlish is not something to be embarrassed about. In fact, it's just the way we Singaporeans speak to bring our meanings across emotionally and efficiently.'

Like the earlier BTS example, this video, too, blurs the boundary between literary creativity and everyday talk. There is perhaps literary creativity in that the video involves actors performing a script, which includes a portrayal of then US President Barack Obama embracing Singlish. There is also everyday creativity in that the uses of Singlish being presented are supposed to be representations of Singaporeans' actual usage. The key point, of course, is that a sharp distinction between these two types of creativity is not really tenable. And as mentioned, the video is produced by US-based Singaporeans. It has both Singaporean and American participants. This additionally blurs the supposedly neat boundaries that correlate specific Circles, communities of speakers and types of creativity.

As with the preceding example, it is also important to give due attention to the roles played by non-human actors. YouTube as an online video sharing platform plays a critical role in allowing for the dissemination of the videos. Because it also allows for fans to upload their comments, the sharing platform is just as critical in letting fans see how other fans are reacting and this creates a feedback loop that establishes both the fact that there are many viewers and reactions as well as a meta-awareness of this fact. Such reactions and awareness of others' reactions help to solidify the cultural reality of Singlish as simultaneously a Singaporean and global phenomenon. As mentioned earlier, it is important not to dismiss these non-human entities (the video as a cultural and technological product that was created and then uploaded, the YouTube platform that allows the sharing of the video as well as the reactions of viewers to the video as well as to comments from other viewers) as mere ancillaries. If the technological affordances provided by these entities were to be discounted, it is not clear that we would be looking at anything like a similar phenomenon.

3.5 Discussion

The foregoing remarks about the two YouTube videos might be dismissed by arguing that it has already long been recognized that the spread of English is accompanied by changes to the language. But the point of this section is not that changes to English are not recognized. Rather, the issue is that the theoretical import of such changes, especially for our understanding of agency and, in the context of the current discussion, creativity in world Englishes, has not been fully appreciated.

It is highly limiting to think of creativity as something exercised simply by speakers from various Circles using different Englishes. This gives us only a partial understanding of the complex networks or assemblages that enable the production and dissemination of language. Taking seriously the roles played by technology and indexicality means acknowledging that: 'Objects, tool, technologies, texts, formulae, institutions and humans are not understood as pertaining to different and incommensurable (semiotic) realms, but as mutually constituting each other' (Farías 2010: 3). In particular, the two examples discussed show that a proper account of the creativity involved cannot simply treat the human actors as shaping the language as they 'creatively' wish. This applies even to V's explicit admission that the proposed use and meaning of 'purple' is something he 'made up'. The modification that V proposes is reliant at the very least on the prior morpho-semantics of 'purple' and the general positive associations that the rainbow carries. It is further enabled by V's celebrity status as a member of BTS and by the availability of social media and various communicative technologies that help spread this nonce formation with the added option of using a purple heart emoji. This contributory role of technology is also clear in the case of the Singlish video. 'Sinful English' is less concerned with proposing a new usage and more interested in challenging negative attitudes about Singlish. But, as an online production, the dissemination of 'Sinful English' relies – perhaps even more so than V's modification of 'purple' – on the affordances of the YouTube platform and the reactions of viewers that the video garners.

These examples demonstrate the assemblage nature of language. As a result, they also allow us to see why questions such as 'Where can we find Korean English/Singlish?' or 'Where can we find English language creativity?' are so problematic. Such locational questions are common enough in the study of world Englishes. Kachru's discussion of 'literary creativity' locates it in the Outer Circles. Widdowson's discussion of 'common talk creativity' is aimed at Kachru's Expanding Circle. There is a distinct geographic bias in these ways of analysing creativity in world Englishes.

But this way of thinking is problematic because it presumes that there can and should be a single definitive answer. In contrast, a posthumanist perspective makes it clear that something like 'Korean English' (whether by this we mean just the use of 'purple' or an assortment of coinages associated with the Hallyu wave or something even more mundane such as the use of English for every communication either in Korea or among Koreans) or 'Sinful English/Singlish' is *multiply* enacted and assembled at concrete local sites' (Farías 2010: 6; emphasis added). It should be clear that what we think of as language is being constantly assembled and reassembled through the joint contributions of humans, technologies and inherited conventions of language use (or indexicalities). As Deleuze and

Parnet (2002: 69) emphasize, an assemblage is 'a multiplicity which is made up of many heterogeneous terms and which establishes liaisons, relations between them, across ages, sexes and reigns – different natures.'

Such constant reassemblings are always ongoing and occurring at multiple sites, which means the analytical focus has to be on the enactments that occur at specific sites and the extent to which such enactments may or may not come to enjoy the labels 'Korean English', 'Hallyu English', 'BTS English', 'Sinful English', 'Singlish', as the case may be. Starting with the presumptive reality of the labels and trying to definitively pin down the locations of the varieties that the labels apparently refer to blinds us to the assemblage nature of language such that the onomastic tail regrettably comes to wag the linguistic dog.

These two examples merely represent the tip of the iceberg when it comes to problematizing the way in which creativity has been approached in the study of world Englishes. Here are three more, briefly described, to indicate just how important it is to start seriously considering creativity from a posthumanist perspective[9].

(i)   Google's Smart Compose is a program that aims to help writers. 'This feature uses machine learning to offer suggestions as you type' (https://support.google.com/docs/answer; accessed 27 January 2021).

(ii) Auto-Tune is an audio processor that measures and alters pitch in vocal and instrumental performances. It is often used to correct off-key singing, thus allowing vocals to be perfectly tuned even though they may have been off-pitch when originally sung by the (human) performer.

(iii) Mercedes-Benz has a voice assistant, named Mercedes. The voice assistant has a female voice. It responds to various driver requests and is activated by being addressed 'Hey, Mercedes'. For example, a driver might simply say 'Hey Mercedes, I'm too cold,' and the ambient lighting around the air vents will glow red and the car's temperature will be raised by a few degrees. (Estrada 2018)

In (i) and (ii), whether it is writing or singing, the relevant program makes an active contribution to the final text or recorded performance. Word processing programs that offer suggestions and auto-correct are of course extremely common, so much so that when communicating via WhatsApp, for example, writers sometimes have to send added messages that correct earlier messages. This is because the latter may contain phrases that were automatically selected or corrected by the program, resulting in texts that the writers did not actually intend. Importantly, the suggested corrections are learned by the program based

---

[9] For a detailed discussion of these examples, see Wee (under preparation).

on the writer's own earlier texts. That is, these are not mechanically selected from a fixed database. Rather, the database itself evolves as a result of the program's own learning via its encounters and interactions with the writer.

As for auto-tuning, one music critic (Reynolds 2018) has described Auto-Tune as 'the fad that just wouldn't fade. Its use is now more entrenched than ever.' Here, the effectiveness of Auto-Tune is its ability to account for the individual performer's departures from the preferred pitch. As with (i), the program's role cannot be dismissed as mechanical. Especially in live performances, Auto-Tune actively processes the performer's singing and adjusts it accordingly. And it can also be used to distort the human voice, lowering or raising the pitch significantly, making the resulting voice sound almost like synthesizer. In both (i) and (ii), the creative products of writing or singing involve the active participation of sophisticated programs.

To repeat Latour's point (see section 1), the writer or singer is not simply using Smart Compose or Auto-Tune as a tool to express of his or her intended message or song. In the same way that a person who picks up a gun 'is not quite the same person as before', a writer or singer who uses Smart Compose or Auto-Tune is not the same as a writer or singer who does not. The results that are enabled are different. And just when a person kills with a gun, 'it is not only the person who kills', likewise, in (i) and (ii), the larger assemblage (of writer/singer plus Smart Compose/Auto-Tune) that writes/sings.

Finally, while (iii) may not be regarded as a typical example of creativity, it is worth noting that the interaction with the voice assistant requires that the speaker address the program in what approximates how that same speaker might informally hail another person ('Hey, . . . '). Significantly, in reacting appropriately, the voice assistant is actually responding to an implicature of the speaker's utterance. That is, the voice assistant has to recognize that 'I'm too cold' is not simply a description of the speaker's own body temperature but is, in fact, a request from the speaker to the voice assistant that it raise the temperature. Here, then, is a case of what might be called 'common talk creativity' since the goal is that it 'serve the entirely normal function of pragmatic use' (Widdowson 2019: 316; see above) – although we have already seen that the distinction between this and literary creativity is problematic. More to the point, whatever kind of creativity we might want to call this, it needs to be attributed to the Mercedes-Benz voice assistant rather than to any human individual.

3.6 Conclusion

A posthumanist perspective on the issue of creativity in world Englishes requires us to recognize the incessant assemblings and reassemblings that are part and parcel of language use. There can be no simple recourse to dichotomies such as 'literary creativity' versus 'common talk creativity', neither can there be easy correlations made between these classifications of creativity and broad sweeps of speakers such as 'Outer Circle', 'Expanding Circle' or 'speakers of English as a lingua franca'.

Rather, by demanding that we give due attention to the distributed nature of agency as well as, concomitantly, the roles played by phenomena such as indexicality and media technologies, it forces us to stop making 'analytical short cuts' because it allows 'other forms of association and assemblages [to] come into view' (Latham and McCormack 2010: 65). What we gain in return for the loss of simple correlations and dichotomies is a more nuanced appreciation of how creativity involves the multiple enactments and assemblages of speakers, language resources and technologies *as well as* a reminder of the complex relationship between these enactments/assemblages and language names.

The theoretical import and value of this gain should not be underestimated. As I have argued elsewhere (Park and Wee 2012, 2013), dominant modern ideologies of language lead us to conceive of language as an entity with clear boundaries, typically correlated with geographical or social boundaries and with an autonomous structure, uniquely definable through a fixed set of formal features. These assumptions guide much of current thinking, research practices, and policy formulation (Pennycook 2007a, b). A posthumanist perspective on world Englishes, then, has the potential to open up a space for critical reflection on the assumptions that guide not only research but also policy formulation. The next section takes up this focus on policy.

4 Language Policy and World Englishes

4.1 Introduction

Spolsky (2004) suggests that language policy consists of three interrelated components: (i) the language practices that speakers actually engage in; (ii) the language ideologies that guide the evaluation of the practices as desirable/undesirable, standard/non-standard, etc.; and (iii) the language management efforts of individuals or groups to modify the practices of targeted speakers. The first two components are necessarily present – since the linguistic behaviour of speakers constitutes their practices and all speakers, whether they are consciously aware of these or not, hold some beliefs or ideologies about their language practices as well as those of others. The third component is optional, since there may not be any actual efforts made to manage language practices.

This way of thinking about language policy is useful. It reminds us of the constant influence of ideologies of various sorts (e.g. beliefs about language, about whether some languages are more valuable than others, about the kinds of people who speak particular languages) on language practices. And it encourages a broader understanding of language policy beyond the official formulations of nation-states since all three components can be found in many different domains such as the family, religion, the workplace, among others.

Nevertheless, there are also limitations. For one, Spolsky's insistence that language management requires that a manager be identified (see section 1) runs counter to the distributed nature of agency. Neither does it give credence to the roles played by non-human actors. At the same time, if we are prepared to acknowledge that agency is distributed and should not be restricted only to human actors, then is it even possible to maintain a distinction between cases where there is language management and cases where there isn't?

In this section, I argue that the distinction is still useful and feasible. It is feasible once we recognize the performance nature of policy. And it is useful because it also helps address a conundrum in the study of world Englishes: how to understand the similarities and differences between English in the Outer Circle and the Expanding Circle. I begin by discussing the performance nature of policy.

4.2 The Performance of Policy

In his theorizing of style, Coupland (2007) recognizes that speakers need to be recognized as engaged in styling even if they are not always highly conscious of what they are doing or how they are projecting themselves. Coupland (2007) thus emphasizes the importance of appreciating that performance can be located on a continuum, ranging from 'mundane' to 'high'.

Mundane performances are routinized, highly conventionalized, and precisely because of the routinization and conventionalization, are typically not even recognized or marked off as performances. In contrast, high performances tend to have the following characteristics (Coupland 2007: 148; emphasis in original):

> [T]hey are scheduled events, typically pre-announced and planned, and therefore programmed. They are temporarily and spatially bounded events, marked off from the routine flow of communicative practice. They are coordinated, in the sense that they rely on specific sorts of collaborative activity, not least in that performers and audience members will establish themselves in these participant roles for the enactment of the performance. High performances are typically also public events, in that membership of the audience will not be especially exclusive. Even if it *is* exclusive, audience members are positioned as parts of a more general social collectivity.

As temporarily and spatially bounded events, high performances are also more likely to be consumed 'as an independent and memorable cultural form' (Coupland and Jaworski 2004: 21). Consequently, they also tend to be 'formally reflexive', demonstrating 'conscious manipulation of the formal feature of the communicative system' (Bauman 1996: 47–8). That is, because high performances are scripted, rehearsed and conducted as events that are marked off, careful attention is often paid not just to the contents of the performances but to the forms.

Policies are rarely thought of in performance terms. Yet, it cannot be denied that when a policy is consciously formulated, its formulation, justification and conveyance to the relevant stakeholders (such as the general public in the case of a national policy) hew closer to the high end of the performance continuum. This is because the formulation, justification and conveyance of a policy are highly reflexive matters, conducted with an awareness of how the policy might be received and where, if necessary, pre-emptive or mitigating actions can be taken to maximize the chance of a positive reception. Here, we can see how the performance continuum provides a way of feasibly maintaining the distinction between language policy with and without management. The former will be located towards the more mundane end of the continuum as they involve language practices that are enacted under the influence of various ideologies without any conscious attempts at management. The latter will be placed towards the high end of the continuum as greater care is taken to lay out and explain the policy in detail.

The fact that performance is understood as being on a continuum is in fact a conceptual advantage because this means that we can recognize language management too as being on a spectrum rather than being a binary matter. There are degrees of management because some aspects of management may be more routinized and established than others. So, even if language management as a whole is to be located towards the high end of the continuum, within the concept of language management, some cases will themselves be more mundane than others. For example, the Singapore government's Speak Good English Movement, launched in 2000, bears similarities to its earlier 1979 Speak Mandarin Campaign (Wee 2006, 2018b). As its predecessor, strategies utilized in the SMC are reapplied in the SGEM. Both campaigns are aimed at encouraging specific uses of language ('Good English' and Mandarin, respectively) whilst discouraging others ('Bad English/Singlish' and Chinese dialects other than Mandarin). Both rely on the argument that the encouraged and discouraged languages cannot co-exist because the presence of the latter makes it difficult to properly learn the former. Both are relaunched annually, each with its own chairman and board and administrative support from the government. Both make use of competitions, games and workshops to raise public awareness and support.

Because both are public activities that involve careful planning and coordination, there is no denying that they are located towards the high end of the performance continuum. But because the strategies developed in the SMC had already been in place for more than twenty years by the time the SGEM was initiated, the SGEM is also more routinized than its predecessor. Such a development is, of course, unsurprising. It would have been more surprising instead if policymakers involved in the SGEM were to completely ignore the lessons learnt and experiences accumulated from the SMC.

This also exemplifies the mobility of policy, albeit in a local context. The more recent effects of mobile policy, or what is sometimes described as 'fast policy transfer' (Peck and Theodore 2015: 429), shifts policy even more towards the high end of the performance continuum. This is because policymakers are increasingly looking at how specific policies that have been formulated elsewhere can be adopted/adapted for their own purposes. As Peck and Theodore (2015: xv) point out, 'policymaking now routinely occurs in knowingly comparative terms, and that best practices from elsewhere pervade so much of the policymaking conversation'. To say that policies are mobile is to recognize that policymakers are increasingly engaged in looking to learn from the recommendations of other policymakers while also sharing their own experiences.

This is not to say that the movement of policies is linear or single-sourced such that it is possible to neatly track a pathway or trail where policy X moves sequentially from policymaker A to policymaker B and so on. Instead, the point here is to acknowledge that (Peck and Theodore 2015: xvi):

> Learning from, and 'referencing', distant models and practices is now commonplace, even as literal replication never really happens. And learning curves can be shortened – sometimes dramatically – if local reform efforts are framed, from the get-go, by a reading of the best-practice literature, by borrowing from a well-known model, or by the importation of authorized designs, expertise, and formulations. It is a widely acknowledged feature of policymaking common sense, in many parts of the world today, that shorthand processes like these, and the various forms of 'speed-up' they imply, have become normalized. 'Traveling policy, like globalization, is nothing new', Catherine Kingfisher (2013: 11) writes, 'nevertheless, it has been accelerating in recent decades to such an extent that it is now ubiquitous, almost mundane'.

Peck and Theodore (2015) discuss the example of New York City's experiment in Conditional Cash Transfers (CCT) to address the problem of urban poverty.

After a review of over sixty antipoverty strategies as well as a scheme from Latin America where payouts to poor families were conditional on 'the maintenance of human-capital building behaviours like school attendance and regular health screening', then Mayor Bloomberg announced that: 'Conditional cash transfer programs have proven effective in countries around the world and, frankly, we need some new ideas here in New York City to fight poverty' (2015: 46). Although the CCT experiment was later deemed a failure (2015: 79), what is of interest to the issue of mobile policy is that 'new ideas' and being 'inspired' by other countries' policies (2015: 60) are not seen as contradictory. Rather, it is generally taken for granted that what works elsewhere will need to be adapted to specific conditions by 'local policy entrepreneurs' (Peck and Theodore 2015: 167). In this way, innovation of a limited kind is built into the ways that policies travel. This is why Peck and Theodore (2015: 4–5) prefer to speak of 'policy mobility and mutation' rather than 'policy transfer'. The latter gives the incorrect impression of unthinking importation and mindless replication.

Thus, when we speak of 'mobile policy' or 'fast policy transfer', we are, in fact, speaking of assemblages being reflexively constituted and reconstituted, thus placing these firmly towards the high end of the performance continuum. A set of ideas, initiatives, documents and human actors are observed to be attempting to effect some change. This is the initial constitution of the policy assemblage. This policy assemblage is considered by policymakers elsewhere to be potentially useful to their own local goals. The policy assemblage is then reconstituted (i.e. adapted to the local context) as a somewhat different policy assemblage. The formulation, justification and conveyance of any policy involves multiple 'policy actors' (McCann and Ward 2011: xiv) such as politicians, policy professionals, practitioners, activists, consultants as well as the documents, presentation slides and communicative technologies that are involved in the policy's construction and dissemination. This distributed nature of agency is very much in line with a posthumanist approach.

4.3 English Language Education: The Common European Framework of Reference for Languages

The foregoing therefore applies also to policy studies concerning world Englishes. Understanding mobile policy as the constitution and reconstitution of policy assemblages allows us to ask which parts of the policy assemblages are intact and which are changed (and to what effect). In the case of English language education, for example, the object of education, English, is something that still tends to be viewed in exonormative terms. The result is a desire, especially for countries located in Kachru's (1986, 1996) Outer and Expanding Circles, to ensure that English is properly taught by adopting an outward orientation not just where the grammatical properties of the language are concerned (Park and Wee 2012) but also as regards the search for how best to go about teaching the language (Holliday 2006). The outward desire to learn from established designs and best practices results in policy mobility with some modifications to facilitate local adaptation.

Consider the Common European Framework of Reference for Languages: Learning, teaching, assessment (CEFR), which was 'designed to provide a transparent, coherent and comprehensive basis for the elaboration of language syllabuses and curriculum guidelines, the design of teaching and learning materials, and the assessment of foreign language proficiency' (www.coe.int /t/dg4/linguistic/cadre1_en.asp; accessed 1 July 2019). The CEFR's website also emphasizes that the framework is not intended to 'offer ready-made solutions but must always be adapted to the requirements of particular contexts.' In this regard, Cambridge University Press has been working with the CEFR to adapt it for English language teachers. Named 'English Profile', the goal is to 'define in more detail the linguistic knowledge typically mastered at each CEFR level – for English' (Cambridge University Press 2013: 4). According to Cambridge University Press, the English Profile website – www .englishprofile.org – gives teachers around the world free access to the findings of various research projects that will help these teachers decide 'which words and phrases ... are typically mastered by learners at each CEFR level' (2013: 8). The CEFR aims to define levels of language proficiency for assessment purposes but it is not simply an assessment tool. It is also concerned with the goals of language learning and teaching so that assessments of proficiency should be contextualized in relation to the former (Read 2014: 13).

While originally intended for Europe, the CEFR is also used in countries such as Taiwan, Japan and China, albeit in different ways. In Taiwan, the government wanted a common standard for evaluating the English proficiency of students, teachers and civil servants. The Taiwanese government treated the CEFR primarily as an assessment tool, mandating that students graduating from an English teacher programme must have a B2, whereas other university graduates must have a B1 (Read 2014: 14). There was no attempt to consider how the specifics of the Taiwanese context – where students don't have the same opportunities to learn or use English as in, say, Europe – should impact on the proficiency assessment (Cheung 2012). As a result, Taiwan's adaptation of the CEFR was characterized by a neglect of CEFR learning and teaching goals.

In Japan, in contrast, the adaptation of the CEFR showed greater sensitivity to local context. A pre-A1 level was added and the A1 level itself divided into sublevels in order to 'differentiate among Japanese learners with a very basic amount of English' (Read 2014: 15). A review of the CEFR descriptors was also undertaken to 'better reflect the degree of difficulty that Japanese learner experienced in performing various communicative tasks in English and the opportunities to use English in the Japanese context' (Read 2014: 15).

In the case of China, the country decided to introduce its own version of the CEFR, the CCFR (the Common Chinese Framework of Reference for Languages). The focus of the CCFR is on the teaching of foreign languages (including English), to stimulate greater reflection among educators as to the pedagogical principles that would be relevant to the country, including 'what the motivations are for Chinese learners to study foreign languages; at which age they should begin foreign language study; what learning resources are available to them; what their cognitive processes are in language learning; which languages (and which variety/-ies of English) should be taught; and what proficiency levels they should aim to achieve' (Read 2014: 15, citing Jin et al. 2014: 23).

Moreover, both Australia and New Zealand have also debated whether to introduce their own national frameworks rather than adopting the CEFR. Significantly, Read (2014: 17) points out that one of the reasons given *against* Australia and New Zealand introducing their own national frameworks is that 'the levels defined by a national framework would not be understood or accepted internationally, so they would need to be benchmarked against a framework like the CEFR anyway to achieve wider currency'.

We see from these examples that, in some cases, the assessment aspect of the CEFR is retained but not the emphasis on learning and teaching goals (Taiwan). In other cases, assessment as well as learning and teaching goals were given attention (Japan). In yet other cases, an awareness of the CEFR led to attempts at creating something that would serve a similar purpose but could be presented as having been created anew, as it were (China, Australia, New Zealand). Language policy tools in these various countries are either adapted or divergent from the pre-existing CEFR. These policy tools are, in the parlance of Deleuze and Guattari, assemblages that evidence different degrees of relative and absolute deterritorialization (section 2). The notion of an assemblage thus provides a way of recognizing the details involved when mobile policy leads to the retention and preservation of some aspects of an earlier policy or, as happens sometimes, a deliberate and conscious desire to depart from a policy predecessor.

When assemblages are constructed with a high degree of deliberation, as tends to be the case when policies are locally formulated with an awareness of how similar policies have been formulated elsewhere, this puts the policy assemblage on the high end of the performance continuum. In this way,

Spolsky's distinction between cases of language policy with management and cases without can be maintained. Cases without language management would be situations where 'ideology operates as "default" policy' (Lo Bianco 2004: 750). Examples might include a father reprimanding his child for using 'bad words' or the management council of a condominium in multilingual Singapore posting signage only in English (without any conscious deliberation as to why this should be acceptable practice).

4.4 The Relationship Between PCEs and Non-PCEs

While an assemblage perspective is of general value to policy study, it also can make a more specific contribution to a particular issue in world Englishes: how to understand the relationship between postcolonial and non-postcolonial Englishes.

A major challenge in accounting for the global spread of English comes from trying to explain the relationship between postcolonial Englishes (PCEs) and non-postcolonial Englishes (non-PCEs). The effects of colonization are by definition relevant to the first group of Englishes and not to the other, thus providing a historical explanation for their differences. Nevertheless, it is acknowledged that in spite of these historical differences, there are current similarities across both groups of Englishes that need to be accounted for (Buschfeld and Kautzsch 2017; Schneider 2014).[10]

For example, Buschfeld and Kautzsch (2017: 113) refer to the 'heterogeneity' that can be 'found in many linguistic contexts, both postcolonial and non-postcolonial alike', attributing these to 'extra-and intra-territorial forces as constantly operating throughout the development of both PCEs and non-PCEs'. And Schneider (2014: 24) refers to English in 'emergent contexts', where it is used in 'expressions of cultural and linguistic hybridity (and contact), "crossing" clear-cut distinctions and traditional taxonomies, defying standard norm orientations, and transcending boundaries of language and nation as distinct entities'. While Schneider (ibid.) describes these as 'distinct from its uses in the Expanding Circle', he also states that: 'I am convinced this is a closely related phenomenon, illustrating the current progression of English into new contexts, related to but going beyond the Expanding Circle, and partly driven by similar factors and motives.'

One attempt at accounting for the similarities is Buschfeld and Kautzsch's (2017) model of extra- and intra-territorial forces (EIFM). The EIFM argues

---

[10] Kachru's (1997) separation of world Englishes into three distinct circles and, in particular, the distinction between Outer and Expanding Circles emphasizes the differences between PCEs and non-PCEs but makes no attempt to account for any similarities.

that both PCEs and non-PCEs develop along the same five phases as those identified by Schneider's (2007) Dynamic Model (DM). The DM actually deals with PCEs and not non-PCEs. It focuses on the changing relationships between the colonial settlers and the indigenous communities, positing five phases (foundation, exonormative stabilization, nativization, endonormative stabilization, differentiation) that cover the development of English in post-colonial contexts, thus connecting the developments of PCEs to their colonial histories as well their later socio-political conditions. The EIFM takes the DM as its starting point and suggests that PCEs and non-PCEs differ in whether their foundation phases involved a period of colonization.

Because the EIFM argues that non-PCEs go through similar phases as PCEs (Buschfeld and Kautzsch 2017: 117 –18), it can therefore be described as adopting a strategy of parallel development in trying to integrate PCEs and non-PCEs. But this parallel development strategy goes too far, neutralizing the differences between PCEs and non-PCEs by trying to absorb them under the same set of phases.[11]

Rather than aiming for parallel development as an explanation, I suggest that convergence can provide a better explanation. Under convergence, both PCEs and non-PCEs can be acknowledged to have had different histories rather than the similar histories that the EIFM is committed to emphasizing. Both PCEs and non-PCEs, however, converge in the era of late modernity given various developments that will be described shortly.

This convergence strategy is also what Schneider (2014) seems to be arguing for in his suggestion that whereas the DM applies to PCEs, in the current era, there is a kind of 'transnational attraction' at work that would account for the similarities between PCEs and non-PCEs. As Schneider (2014: 27–8) puts it:

> In essence, the Dynamic Model is not really, or only to a rather limited extent, a suitable framework to describe this new kind of dynamism of global Englishes. Hence, I propose a different conceptualization for the ongoing dynamism of English . . .
>
> I suggest that the current rush towards and the multiple applications of Englishes on a global scale represent a process best conceptualized as 'Transnational Attraction' – the appropriation of (components of) English(es) for whatever communicative purposes at hand, unbounded by distinctions of norms, nations or varieties. This process is driven predominantly by utilitarian considerations, that is, with users viewing 'English as an economic resource' (Kachru 2005: 91), a symbol of modernity and a stepping stone toward prosperity.

---

[11] See Wee (under preparation) for details.

Transnational attraction is added on to the DM as a 'new kind of dynamism'. It is the perception of English as an 'economic resource' and as 'a symbol of modernity' that leads to the global desire for English. Transnational attraction is a promising notion but characterizing it in terms of utilitarian considerations is problematic for two reasons.

One, utilitarian considerations have long been observed to be relevant to the global spread of English (Phillipson 1992; Pillar and Cho 2013). Certainly, it was a key motivating factor in Singapore's early history for the Eurasian and Peranakan communities becoming early adopters of the language under British colonial rule (Lim 2010; Wee 2010). And it continued to be emphasized after independence as part of Singapore's language policy (Wee 2003). The attraction of English in this case was hardly transnational. So, if the attraction of English is now to be characterized as 'transnational' in the case of *both* PCEs and non-PCES, then we need a stronger explanation as to how the value of English has changed when the perspective is shifted from a domestic to a transnational one. Thus, if transnational attraction is primarily about utilitarian motivations, then such motivations precede the 'current rush towards . . . Englishes'.

Two, as Pennycook (2003) points out, utilitarian considerations are not the only factor at work in the global spread of English. To make his point, he draws on examples from hip hop, suggesting that 'raplish' may be a good example of how English can be appropriated for the expression of a subcultural identity. He cites the lyrics of songs by the Japanese group, Rip Slyme, which contain a mix of Japanese and English (2003: 527). It is clear that Rip Slyme's music is a performance of global and local raplish. There are therefore also matters involving pride and identity aspirations even in the case of the non-PCEs. So, transnational attraction has to also be broader than utilitarianism.

In what follows, I suggest that a focus on mobile policies and their performative nature can help to flesh out Schneider's (2014) notion of transnational attraction and, in so doing, provide us with a better understanding of the relationship between postcolonial Englishes (PCEs) and non-postcolonial Englishes (non-PCEs).

In fact, the discussion in the preceding section of the CEFR already showed how this can be done. We saw that the countries that contemplated adapting the CEFR or producing their own version included those whose Englishes would be classified as non-PCEs (Taiwan, Japan, China) as well as PCEs (Australia, New Zealand). The influence of the CEFR cuts across the non-PCE/PCE distinction. The era of mobile policy, in this case, the global awareness of the CEFR and the pressure in various countries to respond in one way or another, has neutralized the non-PCE/PCE distinction. This accounts for the observation that similarities between PCEs and non-PCEs is a relatively recent phenomenon since it is only in recent decades that 'traveling policy' has accelerated to become a significant aspect of policymaking.

Let us now consider another example in greater detail, one that concerns global rankings and the pursuit of English. The CEFR mobile policy example can be viewed as illustrating 'horizontal' performativity. Policymakers are looking at the practices of policymakers elsewhere ('peers') and making decisions about whether and how to adopt the ideas and practices gleaned from elsewhere. We now look at 'vertical' performativity, where a central monitor evaluates and ranks the levels of English competence across a group of evaluated entities. I present the examples first before explaining why the use of rankings, too, is a matter of performativity.

There are many rankings being produced that claim to measure how widely used English is in a given industry, country or city, as well as the linguistic competence of the respective populations. While such rankings are not strictly speaking a part of English language education, they nevertheless constitute part of the larger ecosystem within which English language education policies and activities exist. And their influence on the importance that is accorded to English language education – with concomitant consequences for the allocation of funding and other resources, the politicization of English as a utility that families expect governments and schools to provide – cannot be underestimated.

Consider, for example, that there is a map produced of the 'Top Ten English Speaking Countries' where 'Top countries include the USA, UK, India, Philippines etc.'[12] While it is, of course, not impossible that similar maps could be produced for 'Chinese Speaking Countries' or 'Italian Speaking Countries', these are not as likely simply because as *the* global language, it is English whose presence in different countries becomes a matter of global interest. Notice, therefore, that it is not simply a matter of quantifying the number of speakers in each country, but a matter of ranking as well ('The Top Ten ... '), thus implicating that having as many speakers as possible is something that each country might aspire towards.

As a second example, consider that the GlobalEnglish Corporation (www .GlobalEnglish.com)[13] releases an annual Business English Index, where

---

[12] Maps World, www.mapsofworld.com/world-top-ten/countries-with-most-english-language-speaker-map.html; accessed 16 September 2014.

[13] Yahoo! Finance, 23 April 2013, http://finance.yahoo.com/news/globalenglish-releases-business-english-index-120300860.html; accessed 16 September 2014.

industries and countries with the highest and lowest BEI scores were ranked. The 2013 BEI results are shown below.

4.4.1 Industries With the Highest and Lowest BEI Scores

Top five industries		Bottom five industries	
Aerospace/defence	6.63	Real estate/construction	2.82
Professional services	6.22	Govt/ed/non-profit	3.18
Technology	5.72	Media/comm/entertainment	3.20
Financial services	4.93	Energy/utilities	3.96
Retail	4.92	Auto/transportation	3.99

4.4.2 Countries With the Highest and Lowest BEI Scores

Top five countries		Bottom five countries	
Philippines	7.95	Honduras	2.92
Norway	7.06	Columbia	3.05
Netherlands	7.03	Saudi Arabia	3.14
United Kingdom	6.81	Mexico	3.14
Australia	6.78	El Salvador and Chile	3.24

As a company, GlobalEnglish undoubtedly has an undoubted vested interested in stoking the desire for improving English language skills since it is in the business of providing business English to help 'improve the way your business communicates, collaborates and operates'.[14] Nevertheless, this desire itself for improving English is a very real one that exists independently of the company. Thus, in the 2012 BEI, the Philippines was also ranked highest and this led to a clear sense of national pride (Mendoza 2012):

> Well, people will now have to think twice before mocking Pinoys' use of the English language. The Philippines was named the world's best country in business English proficiency, even beating the United States, according to a recent study by GlobalEnglish Corporation . . . For 2012, results showed that from 76 represented countries worldwide, only the Philippines attained a score above 7.0, 'a BEI level within range of a high proficiency that indicates an ability to take an active role in business discussions and perform relatively complex tasks'.

---

[14] Pearson English; www.globalenglish.com/purchase/business; accessed 16 September 2014.

As a third example, consider that when Sweden was named a high English-proficiency country, this, too, led to a boosting of national pride:[15]

> It's time to stop teasing the Swedes for their *Swenglish*, as they've yet again topped English Proficiency Index from language education company Education First (EF), which was founded in Sweden.
>
> 'It's the second time in a row, so I guess we're a bit used to it, but of course it's really neat that we are the world leaders when it comes to speaking English', Sine Ejsing, Country Manager of EF Sweden, told The Local.
>
> The language test quizzed 750,000 people from 60 countries around the world, and the Nordic nations scored prominently, with Norway placing second, followed by the Netherlands, Estonia, Denmark, Austria and Finland.

These various rankings are clear demonstrations of Foucauldian surveillance technologies at work. A central monitoring institution creates awareness among the entities that are being ranked (Wee 2011: 45). Especially in the case of rankings that are updated and published publicly on a regular basis such as annually or biannually, this provides a means for tracking and comparing the performance of the ranked entities over time. As the peer entities monitor one another's progress (or lack thereof), those who manage to 'outdo' their competitors evince pride in their achievement should they manage to move up the rankings to improve their positioning. In this regard, competitions constitute just the kind of circumstances under which self-objectification and hence, reflexivity, arises. Entities involved in competition are inevitably aware of how they stand in relation to other potential competitors, not least because the competitive gaze involves competitors constantly sizing one another up. This sense of competitive pride is particularly clear in the following report,[16] which describes Malaysia as 'edging out Singapore' in an English skills test:

> Malaysia took top marks in an English skills test given to Asian nations, narrowly edging out Singapore, where English is one of the official national languages.
>
> The Philippines, where English is also spoken as a national language, was excluded from the 60 countries and regions whose English skills were measured by international education company EF Education First for the 2013 English Proficiency Index.

---

[15] The Local: Sweden's News in English, 7 November 2013 (no author); 'Swedes "best in the world" at English – again'; www.thelocal.se/20131107/swedes-ranked-again-best-world-english; accessed 16 September.

[16] GUESS WHAT! Malaysians are the BEST English speakers in Asia', 19 December 2013, no author; www.malaysia-chronicle.com/index.php?optionwww.malaysia-chronicle.com/index.php?option= com_k2&view=item&id=202652:guess-what-malaysians-are-the-best-english-speakers-in-asia-ranking&Itemid=2#ixzz3DG7q2CoK; accessed 14 September 2014.

In the examples presented above, the competition involves different countries – and to a lesser extent, different industries – being gauged on their relative competencies vis-à-vis English. And there is a clear economic motivation behind these comparisons, since English is ideologically widely linked to economic success and global competitiveness. This emerges with particular clarity when we consider the EF English Proficiency Index, which claims to provide an answer to the question 'Which cities in the world speak the best English?' (www.ef.com/epi; accessed 16 September 2014). The top five cities, according to this Index, are:

Zurich 64.67
Frankfurt 64.09
Munich 61.86
Moscow 61.31
Geneva 61.31

More interestingly, the Index also provides brief commentaries that serve to make explicit both the economic and competitive natures of the rankings, as well as the key role that English is presumed to play in influencing how the various cities are ranked, as the following demonstrate:

> Paris, Rome, Madrid and Barcelona are handicapped their bid to keep ahead with other global cities by their poor English compared with other European cities such as Zurich and Berlin.
> There are wide disparities between leading cities of the BRIC countries, the developing nations – Brazil, Russia, India and China – competing to be future economic superpowers. Moscow comes 4th and St Petersburg 7th, but Beijing and Shanghai are 19th and 20th, with Rio de Janeiro and Sao Paulo only 21st and 22nd.

We have seen from the above examples that competence in English can be ideologized as an ability that can be measured and ranked. Furthermore, there is demonstrable pride in doing well in these rankings and, concomitantly, anxiety when doing poorly. Of particular relevance to the issue of the relationship between PCEs and non-PCEs, it is worth noting that the countries listed in the rankings – India, China, the Philippines, Singapore, Malaysia, Sweden, Russia –cut across the distinction and can even include the United Kingdom. The point is that rankings such as these do not care about the distinction between PCEs and non-PCEs. The distinction is irrelevant when the goal of the rankings is to place different countries on a scale of English competence.

The production of the rankings, as we have seen, elicits responses from those being ranked. These responses generally take pride in doing well in rankings. As shown in Wee (2011: 52), entities do not really have much of a choice about whether or not to participate in such rankings. Being left out of such rankings would be interpreted negatively by those readers (e.g. business organizations, politicians, investors) for whom such lists are produced. It might even be interpreted as a sign that the entity is so bad at whatever attribute is being ranked as to not warrant being on the list at all. And of course, there is nothing to stop the monitoring institution from including the entity on its rankings, in spite of any protestations. These rankings demonstrate that ranked entities are (Wee 2011: 44–5):

> [A]ware that they are being ranked, the issue here is not uncertainty about whether or not they are monitored. Rather, it is the awareness of being constantly monitored, particularly in the case of 'prestigious' lists that may be generated on a regular basis, such as annual lists.

Just as with the CEFR (see preceding section), the global rankings of English also present us with policymaking as performance, one that is located towards the high end of the performance continuum. As different countries strive to improve or at least attain some respectable showing on ranked lists, these activities can easily lead to a convergence – resulting from the mobility of policy but also from an awareness of what kinds of specific criteria might be employed by a monitoring institution as it decides on specific placements. For example, De Costa, Park and Wee (2019) show that such rankings can create intense pressure among organizations, countries and industries to improve their linguistic capabilities and, in particular, can be compelled 'to adopt the entrepreneurial image of personhood promoted by such ideological representations' of language competence.

The pressure to perform well on rankings is exacerbated by the pervasive influence of audit culture. Audit culture refers to the way in which principles of financial auditing come to serve as a prevalent logic for ensuring economic efficiency and regulatory accountability across multiple domains of society (Strathern 2000). Power (1994: 1) describes an 'audit explosion' in which he observes that:

> In addition to financial audits, there are now environmental audits, value for money audits, management audits, forensic audits, data audits, intellectual property audits, medical audits, teaching audits, technology audits, stress audits, democracy audits and many others besides. More generally, the spread of audits and other quality assurance initiatives means that many individuals and organisations now find themselves subject to audit for the first time and, notwithstanding protest and complaint, have come to think of themselves as auditees

Audit culture leads to a greater degree of reflexivity that drives organizations to pursue recognizable 'best practices'. The emphasis that auditing regimes place on competition and quantitative benchmarking tends to result in increased convergence instead of diversity of models, as competing institutions adopt similar strategies and modes of self-presentation. Van Doorn (2014: 362; see also Power 2003: 191) observes how audits tend to rely on rankings and ratings where the auditees are competitively evaluated against one another. Audit culture thus both facilitates and is facilitated by policy mobility given the emphasis on 'learning from' and 'referencing' distant models (Peck and Theodore 2015: xvi; see above). For this reason, policy mobility serves as a basis for prescriptive convergence. As Strathern (1997: 312) argues:

> The auditors' interest is not in producing an 'organizational model' in the sense of the model of an ongoing organization with its own characteristics ... They measure the institution as an organization according to pre-set criteria of what an efficient organization would look like ... [that is] by the degree to which the institution conforms to certain standard models (representations) of organizations that achieve their goals ... the extent to which the institution looks like other institutions that fall into this class, and thus can be described as conforming.

The notion of language management thus returns with even greater force and relevance in the case of global rankings of English language competence. A strong orientation to comparison and competition, prominence of best practices and performance metrics, the pressure to conform to prescriptive models and the dominating influence of audit culture – all these serve not only to locate policy towards the high end of the performance continuum, they also show why there might be policy convergence that cuts across the PCE/non-PCE distinction.

4.5 Conclusion

Language policies are complex geopolitical assemblages. Nevertheless, they can be highly routinized or performed with little actual deliberation or actual awareness, so that there is no language management to speak of. Often, however, they are formulated with care, drawing on similar policies that have been formulated elsewhere.

In the case of a global language such as English, the policy assemblages involved provide us with insights into the evolving relationship between PCEs and non-PCEs, including why they should happen to be converging. Particularly in an age when audit culture presses policymakers towards greater accountability, which can include global comparisons so as to justify 'best practices', approaching policy as both assemblage and performance helps to flesh out what Schneider (2014) calls transnational attraction.

If transnational attraction merely refers to the pursuit of English, either for utilitarian or identity reasons, then it does not really clarify why we should be observing convergences between PCEs and non-PCEs. English has spread across the globe because it is used in many different countries and communities, but this means the emergence of many different varieties of English (Kachru 1986) that serve a range of communicative and communal needs (Widdowson 1994).

This section has shown that the centripetal force in transnational attraction is not only the English language per se. It is the range of mobile policies that are assembled and reassembled in multiple settings, it is the centralized monitors such as ranking institutions that assess and compile the English language competence of ranked entities and, perhaps most importantly, it is the high performance that results from an awareness that organizations and countries are being compared with other organizations or countries.

5 Conclusion: Linguistics for the Ontologically Curious

5.1 Introduction

This Element has argued for a posthumanist approach to world Englishes. By focusing on creativity and language policy, it has highlighted the value of thinking in terms of assemblages and demonstrated how this way of thinking can provide interesting insights and more nuanced understandings of the issues involved.

In this concluding section, I want to emphasize that, whether or not ideas such as posthumanism or the assemblage find purchase, it is important to give attention to the issue of language ontology. I begin by distinguishing between approaches that are ontologically naive and approaches that are ontologically curious.

5.2 Ontological Naivety

Ontological naivety is exemplified by John Honey's (1997) assertions about standard English. Honey's goal is to promote and protect some named varieties of English (particularly his own understanding of what constitutes 'standard English) while disparaging other ('non-standard') varieties – but without seriously inquiring into the bases by which such varieties are reified. Thus, consider the following statement from Honey (1997: 81):

> The study of school text books for spelling, reading, writing, and speaking make it abundantly clear that between the sixteenth and the beginning of the nineteenth centuries there was an ever more widely held notion of a standard form of English, all the elements of which were realistically accessible through book-learning.

Honey also insists on 'educatedness' (1997: 235) as the hallmark of standard English speakers, although he also allows for other, sufficiently 'high status' individuals or circumstances (1997: 161–2):

> [G]raduation from (often famous) universities, or literary reputation, or the ability in all other respects to use the language in highly acceptable ways – or [people] who are in some way other high-status figures (like royalty).

Two things should be noted about Honey's assertions. One, despite his acknowledgement of social and historical change (i.e. the references to time periods), the statement carries the suggestion that once the notion of 'a standard form of English' emerged and became 'widely held', questions about the social, historical and political factors that played a role in its emergence, continued legitimacy and even possible dismantling no longer carry any import.

Two, it is not the case that Honey is not aware that the legitimacy of the notion of a standard might be challenged. His references to 'enemies' of standard English (the word actually appears in the subtitle of his book) bears testament to this awareness. However, he seems to consider any serious academic questioning about the nature of standard English as evidence of the 'enemies' at work.

This is why it is not inaccurate to consider his approach ontologically naive. Ontological naivety here does not refer to the simplistic assumption that English somehow appears fully formed, perhaps as a gift of divinity. That would likely be a strawman since it is not clear that anyone actually holds such a position. Rather, it refers to the refusal to engage with inconvenient questions of ontology because these would undermine whatever linguistic agenda is being pursued. And as Crowley (1999: 272; emphasis added) observes in his comments on Honey's assertions regarding standard English:

> Its danger lies in the presupposition that there is in some sense standard (written) English and standard (spoken) English and that they share a common structure. It is as though standard English were an ideal form of the language which is realised in practice by 'the best' users of English in the forms of standard written and spoken English.

This presupposition that the structure of standard English is common to both written and spoken forms and that it can be found in the language practices of the 'best users' is such an article of faith that those who dare subject this presupposition to scrutiny are even accused by Honey of attempting to engage in a conspiracy to impede the cognitive and social progress of certain segments of society. What Honey fails (or does not want) to appreciate is that his notion of standard English is an assemblage and hence not much different from the ways in which Tinglish or Thaiglish are assembled (see section 2).

5.3 Ontological Curiosity

An ontologically curious position, in contrast, takes seriously rather than skirts the question of just how languages, including standard English and its non-standard counterparts, are constituted. It avoids taking the name of a variety at face value and it most certainly refrains from accusing those who wish to inquire into the nature of a variety as being 'enemies'.

This is important because there is a tendency to use a language name such as 'standard English' as if it referred unproblematically to a set of language practices while ignoring the ideological work (sometimes explicitly, sometimes implicitly) that goes into linking the name to the practices (Park and Wee 2012). By ignoring the ideological assumptions that link the name to the practices, there is a serious danger of treating a named variety such as standard English as a stable product, that is, the uncritical use of the name gives the impression that the name refers to a clearly defined and clearly understood bounded and stable set of languages practices.

The problem here is that the variation and changeability in language practices, as well as the ideological influences that lead some speakers and institutions to accept certain practices as 'standard English' while rejecting others then go un-interrogated. This is a point that Schneider (2011: 155) makes in his discussion of English in Asia, where he notes that a label like 'Chinese English', 'unless understood very loosely and non-technically, implies more homogeneity than is warranted'.

The ramifications of a failure to be ontologically curious can be significant for scholarly attempts to better understand the nature of, among other things, standards in English. And of course, discussions about whose standards to adopt or who decides on what the standards ought to be can be highly consequential for many individuals and communities. Those who are seen as failing to meet the standards can be denied further opportunities in education or the workplace (Park 2013) – which is why Honey (see above) has a vested interest in defending his particular assemblage of standard English. In addition to the question of standards in English, we have also seen that the issue of language ontology is central to how we want to understand the rising use of automation in communication, the nature of language and creativity and the relationship between PCEs and non-PCEs, among others.

5.4 Conclusion

This Element began with the argument that there are 'regimes of truth' about language that are in urgent need of critical re-evaluation. Assumptions about how language relates to agency and community are deeply ingrained into current academic orthodoxy. So much so that the naming of language varieties is all too often treated as an innocent act of identification, of making reference to an independently existing object, rather than being seen as a socio-political act of reifying (and hence, assembling) some phenomenon. Thus, Park and Wee (2013: 352) point out:

> Our research habitus that presumes language as bounded, enumerable, discrete varieties leads us to consider names as mere labels for pre-existing entities. Under this view, the linguist' s assigning of names to certain sets of linguistic practices is no more than a neutral act of reference; the linguist is in no way interfering into the reality being studied, which makes this research activity completely objective and scientific. But . . . this obscures issues of descriptive adequacy and commensurability of labels, and more importantly, the fact that names are socially constituted.

I have in response proposed that there are significant merits to adopting a posthumanist approach and, as part of that approach, to viewing language as an assemblage. But whether or not these specific proposals are utilized, I would urge that more attention be given to the matter of language ontology than has so far been the case, rather than any dismissal or trivialization of its relevance and import.

References

Ahearn, L. (2001). Agency. In Alessandro Duranti, ed., *Key Terms in Language and Culture*. Oxford: Blackwell, pp. 7–10.

Bakhtin, M. (1981). *The Dialogic Imagination*. Translated by C. Emerson and M. Holquist. Austin: University of Texas Press.

Barad, K. (2007). *Meeting the Universe Halfway: Quantum Physics and the Entanglement of Matter and Meaning*. Durham: Duke University Press.

Bates, E. and MacWhinney, B. (1987). Competition, Variation and Language Learning. In B. MacWhinney, ed., *Mechanisms of Language Acquisition*. Hillsdale: Lawrence Erlbaum, pp. 157–93.

Bauman, R. (1996). Transformations of the Word in the Production of Mexican Festival Drama. In M. Silverstein and G. Urban, eds., *Natural Histories of Discourse*. Chicago: University of Chicago Press, pp. 301–27.

Bennett, J. (2010). *Vibrant Matter: A Political Ecology of Things*. Durham: Duke University Press.

Blommaert, J. (2005). *Discourse: A Critical Introduction*. Cambridge: Cambridge University Press.

Blommaert, J. (2010). *The Sociolinguistics of Globalization*. Cambridge: Cambridge University Press.

Blommaert, J. (2016). From Mobility to Complexity in Sociolinguistic Theory and Method. In N. Coupland, ed., *Sociolinguistics: Theoretical debates*. Cambridge: Cambridge University Press, pp. 242–59.

Blommaert, J. and Rampton, B. (2016). Language and Superdiversity. In K. Arnaut, J. Blommaert, B. Rampton and M. Spotti, eds., *Language and Superdiversity*. New York: Routledge, pp. 21–48.

Bonta, M. and Protevi, J. (2004). *Deleuze and Geophilosophy: A Guide and Glossary*. Edinburgh: Edinburgh University Press.

Bourdieu, P. (1977). *Outline of a Theory of Practice*. Cambridge: Cambridge University Press.

Buschfeld, S. and Kautzsch, A. (2017). Towards an Integrated Approach to Postcolonial and Non-Postcolonial Englishes. *World Englishes*, 36(1), 104–26.

Cheung, H. (2012). Academic Perspectives from Taiwan. In M. Byram and L. Parmenter, eds., *The Common European Framework of Reference: The globalisation of language education policy*. Bristol: Multilingual Matters, pp. 224–30.

Conquergood, D. (1997). Street Literacy. In J. Flood, S. Brice Heath and D. Lapp, eds., *Handbook of Research on Teaching Literacy through the*

Communicative and Visual Arts. New York: Simon & Schuster, pp. 354–75.

Corti, K. and Gillespie, A. (2015). Revisiting Milgram's Cyranoid Method: Experimenting with hybrid human agents. *Journal of Social Psychology*, 155(1), 30–56.

Coupland, N. (2007). *Style.* Cambridge: Cambridge University Press.

Coupland, N. and Jaworski, A. (2004). Sociolinguistic Perspectives on Metalanguage. In A. Jaworski, N. Coupland and D. Galasinksi, eds., *Metalanguage: Social and ideological perspectives.* Berlin: Mouton.

Crowley, T. (1999). Curiouser and Curiouser: Falling Standards in the Standard English Debate. In T. Bex and R. J. Watts, eds., *Standard English. The Widening Debate.* London: Routledge, pp. 271–82.

De Costa, P., Park, J. and Wee, L. (2019). Linguistic Entrepreneurship as Affective Regime: Organizations, audit culture, and second/foreign language education policy. *Language Policy*, 18, 387–406.

DeLanda, M. (2006). *A New Philosophy of Society: Assemblage Theory and Social Complexity.* London: Continuum.

Deleuze, G. and Guattari, F. (1987). *A Thousand Plateaus.* Translated by B. Massumi. London: Athlone Press.

Deleuze, G. and Parnet C. (2002) [1977] *Dialogues II.* Translated by H. Tomlinson and B. Habberjam. New York: Continuum.

Durkheim, E. (1933). *Division of Labor in Society.* New York: Macmillan.

Eckert, P. (2008). Variation and the Indexical Field. *Journal of Sociolinguistics*, 12, 453–76.

Eckert, P. (2012). Three Waves of Variation Study: The emergence of meaning in the study of sociolinguistic variation. *Annual Review of Anthropology*, 41, 87–100.

Edwards, J. (2012). *Multilingualism: Understanding Linguistic Diversity.* London: Continuum.

Estrada, Z. (2018). Mercedes uses its new car to launch yet another voice assistant. *The Verge.* 10 January 2018, www.theverge.com/2018/1/10/ 16872494/mercedes-voice-assistant-infotainment-ux-ces-2018; accessed 27 September 2019.

Faist, T. (2000). *The Volume and Dynamics of International Migration and Transnational Social Spaces.* Oxford: Oxford Scholarship Online.

Farías, I. (2010). Introduction: Decentring the Object of Urban Studies. In I. Farías and T. Bender, eds., *Urban Assemblages: How actor-network theory changes urban studies.* New York: Routledge, pp. 1–24.

Fillmore, C. J., Kay, P. and O'Connor, M. C. (1988). Regularity and Idiomaticity in Grammatical Constructions. *Language*, 64, 501–38.

Foucault, M. (1977). The Political Function of the Intellectual. *Radical Philosophy*, 17, 12–14.

Galeon, D. (2017). Our computers are learning how to code themselves. 24 February 2017. Futurism, https://futurism.com/4-our-computers-are-learning-how-to-code-themselves; accessed 13 September 2019.

Gibson, J. J. (1966). *The Senses Considered as Perceptual Systems*. London: Allen & Unwin.

Gibson, J. J. (1979). *The Ecological Approach to Visual Perception*. Boston: Houghton Mifflin Harcourt.

Giddens, A. (1984). *The Constitution of Society*. Cambridge: Polity Press.

Giddens, A. (1990). *The Consequences of Modernity*, Cambridge: Polity Press.

Giddens, A. (2002). *Runaway World: How Globalization is Reshaping Our Lives*, 2nd ed. London: Profile Books.

Goffman, E. (1956). *The Presentation of Self in Everyday Life*. New York: Doubleday.

Goldberg, A. (2005). *Constructions at Work*. Oxford: Oxford University Press.

Hagens, S. A. (2005). *Attitudes Toward Konglish of South Korean Teachers of English in the Province of Jeollanamdo*. Dissertation. Brock University, Canada.

Haggerty, K. D. and Ericson, R. V. (2000). The Surveillant Assemblage. *British Journal of Sociology*, 51(4), 605–22.

Haraway, D. (1991). *Simians, Cyborgs and Women*. London: Free Association Books.

Haraway, D. (2016). *A Cyborg Manifesto*. Minneapolis: University of Minnesota Press.

Hawkins, R. (2001). *Second Language Syntax: A Generative Introduction*. Oxford: Blackwell.

Hazard, S. (2013). The Material Turn in the Study of Religion. *Religion and Society*, 4, 58–78.

Heller, M. (2008). Language and the Nation-State: Challenges to sociolinguistic theory. *Journal of Sociolinguistics*, 12(4), 504–24.

Herschensohn, J. (2000). *The Second Time Around: Minimalism and Second Language Acquisition*. Amsterdam: John Benjamins.

Hilles, S. (1987). Interlanguage and Pro-Drop Parameter. *Second Language Research*, 3(1), 33–52.

Hoffman, T. and Trousdale, G. (2013). Construction Grammar: Introduction. In T. Hoffman and G. Trousdale, eds., *The Oxford Handbook of Construction Grammar*. Oxford: Oxford University Press, pp. 1–12.

Holliday, A. (2006). Native-Speakerism. *ELT Journal*, 60(4), 385–7.

Holston, J. (1999). *Cities and Citizenship*. Durham: Duke University Press.

Honey, J. (1997). *Language Is Power: The Story of Standard English and its Enemies.* London: Faber & Faber.

Hopper, P. and Traugott, E. (1993). *Grammaticalization.* Cambridge: Cambridge University Press.

Jenkins, J. (2007). *English as a Lingua Franca: Attitude and Identity.* Oxford: Oxford University Press.

Jin, Y., Wu, Z., Alderson, C. and Song W. (2014). Developing the Common Chinese Framework of Reference for Languages: Challenges at macro and micropolitical levels. Paper presented at the Language Testing Research Colloquium, Amsterdam, the Netherlands, June 4–6.

Jing, X. and Zuo, N. (2006). Chinglish in the Oral Work of Non-English Majors. *CELEA Journal*, 29(4).

Kachru, B. (1985). Standards, Codification, and Sociolinguistic Realism: The English Language in the Outer Circle. In R. Quirk and H. G. Widdowson, eds., *English in the World: Teaching and learning the language and literatures.* Cambridge:Cambridge University Press, pp. 11–30.

Kachru, B. (1986). *The Alchemy of English: The Spread, Functions and Models of Non-Native Englishes.* Pergamon.

Kachru, B. (1995). Transcultural Creativity in World Englishes and Literary Canons. In G. Cook and B. Seidlhofer, eds. *Principle and Practice in Applied Linguistics: Studies in honour of H. G. Widdowson.* Oxford: Oxford University Press, pp. 271–87.

Kachru, B. (1997). World Englishes and English-Using Communities. *Annual Review of Applied Linguistics*, 17, 66-87.

Kachru, B. (2005). *Asian Englishes Beyond the Canon.* Hong Kong: Hong Kong University Press.

Kachru, B. and C. Nelson. (1996). World Englishes. In S. McKay and N. Hornberger, eds., *Sociolinguistics in Language Teaching.* Cambridge: Cambridge University Press, pp. 71–102.

Kay, P. and Fillmore, C. J. (1999). Grammatical Constructions and Linguistic Generalisations: The 'What's X doing Y?' construction. *Language*, 75, 1–33.

Kennedy, P. (2001). Introduction: Globalization and the Crisis of Identities? In P. Kennedy and C. J. Danks, eds., *Globalization and National Identities: Crisis or opportunity?* New York: Palgrave, pp. 1–28.

Kirkpatrick, A. (2014). *World Englishes. The Routledge Companion to English Studies Routledge*, www.routledgehandbooks.com/doi/10.4324/9781315852515.ch3; accessed 31 December 2019.

Krashen, S. (1977). Some Issues Relating to the Monitor Model. In H. Brown, C. Yorio and R. Crymes, eds., *On TESOL '77.* Washington: TESOL, pp. 144–58.

Labov, W. (1963). The Social Motivation of a Sound Change. *Word*, 18, 1–42.

Labov, W. (1972). *Sociolinguistic Patterns*. Philadelphia: University of Pennsylvania Press.

Laitin, D. (2000). What is a Language Community? *American Journal of Political Science*, 44(1), 142–55.

Lamb, R. (2015). Echoborg: The computer controls you. 11 August 2015. *Stuff to Blow Your Mind*, www.stufftoblowyourmind.com/podcasts/echoborg-the-computer-controls-you.htm; accessed 20 May 2017.

Lanza, E. (2004). *Language Mixing in Infant Bilingualism*, new ed. Oxford: Oxford University Press.

Larsen-Freeman, D. and Cameron, L. (2008). *Complex Systems and Applied Linguistics*. Oxford: Oxford University Press.

Latham, A. and McCormack, D. (2011). Globalizations Big and Small: Notes on urban studies, actor-network theory, and geographical scale. In I. Farías and T. Bender, eds., *Urban Assemblages*. London: Routledge, pp. 53–72.

Latour, B. (1999). *Pandora's Hope: Essays on the Reality of Science Studies*. Cambridge, MA: Harvard University Press.

Lee, J. H. X. and Nadeau, K. M. (2011). *Encyclopedia of Asian American Folklore and Folklife*, Vol 1. California: ABC-CLIO.

Lim, L. (2010). Peranakan English. In D. Schreier, P. Trudgill, E. Schneider and J. Williams, eds., *The Lesser-Known Varieties of English*. Cambridge: Cambridge University Press, pp. 327–47.

Lo Bianco, J. (2004) Language Planning as Applied Linguistics In A. Davies and C. Elder, eds., *Handbook of Applied Linguistics*. Oxford: Blackwell, pp. 738–62.

Maley, A. (2010). The Reality of EIL and the Myth of ELF. In C. Gagligardi and A. Maley, eds., *EIL, ELF, Global English: Teaching and learning issues*. Bern: Peter Lang, pp. 25–44.

Matras, Y. (2009). *Language Contact*. Cambridge: Cambridge University Press.

McCann,E. and Ward,K., eds. (2011). *Mobile Urbanism*. Minneapolis: University of Minnesota Press.

McLaughlin, B. (1987). *Theories of Second Language Learning*. London: Edward Arnold.

Mendes, A. (2020). Verdant Vernaculars: Corsican environmental assemblages. *Journal of Linguistic Anthropology*, 30/2, 156–78.

Mendoza, S. (2012). PH: World's best country in Business English. *Yahoo! Southeast Asia Newsroom*, 25 April 2012, https://sg.news.yahoo.com/ph-world-s-best-country-in-business-english.html; accessed 28 October 2020.

Mesthrie, R. (1992). *English in Language Shift: The History, Structure and Sociolinguistics of South African Indian English*. Cambridge: Cambridge University Press.

Muniandy, M. K., Nair, G. K. S., Shanmugam, S. K. K., Ahmad, I. and Mohamed Noor N. B. (2010). Sociolinguistic Competence and Malaysian Students' English Language Proficiency. *English Language Teaching*, 3(3), 145–51.

Nash, R. (1970). Spanglish: Language contact in Puerto Rico. *American Speech*, 45, 223–33.

Park, J. (2013). Metadiscursive Regimes of Diversity in a Multinational Corporation. *Language in Society*, 42, 1–21.

Park, J. and Wee, L. (2011). A Practice-Based Critique of English as a Lingua Franca. *World Englishes*, 30(3), 360–74.

Park, J. and Wee, L. (2012). *Markets of English*. London: Routledge.

Park, J. and Wee, L. (2013). Linguistic Baptism and the Disintegration of ELF. *Applied Linguistics Review*, 4(2), 339–59.

Parsons, T. (1937). *The Structure of Social Action*. New York: Free Press.

Parsons, T. (1960). *Structure and Process in Modern Society*. New York: Free Press.

Parsons, T. (1971). *The System of Modern Societies*. Englewood Cliffs: Prentice Hall.

Pavlenko, A. (2017). Superdiversity and Why it Isn't: Reflections on Terminological Innovation and Academic Branding. In B. Schmenk, S. Breidbach and L. Kuster, eds., *Sloganizations in Language Education Discourse*. Clevedon: Multilingual Matters, pp. 142–68.

Peck, J. and Theodore, N. (2015). *Fast Policy*. Minneapolis: University of Minnesota Press.

Pennycook, A. (2003). Global Englishes, Rip Slyme, and Performativity. *Journal of Sociolinguistics*, 7(4), 513–33.

Pennycook, A. (2007a). The Myth of English as an International Language. In S. Makoni and A. Pennycook, eds., *Disinventing and Reconstituting Languages*. Clevedon: Multilingual Matters, pp. 90–115.

Pennycook, A. (2007b). *Global Englishes and Transcultural Flows*. London: Routledge.

Pennycook, A. (2008). Linguistic Landscape and the Transgressive Semiotics of Graffiti. In E. Shohamy and D. Gorter, eds., *Linguistic Landscapes: Expanding the Scenery*. New York: Routledge, pp. 302–12.

Pennycook, A. (2016). Mobile Times, Mobile Terms: The Trans-Super-Poly-Metro Movement. In N. Coupland, ed., *Sociolinguistics: Theoretical debates*. Cambridge: Cambridge University Press, pp. 201–16.

Pennycook, A. (2018). *Posthumanist Applied Linguistics*. London: Routledge.

Perrons, D. (2004). *Globalization and Social Change*. London/New York: Routledge.

Phillipson, R. (1992). *Linguistic Imperialism*. Oxford: Oxford University Press.

Pierce, J. E. (1971). Culture, Diffusion and Japlish. *Linguistics*, 9, 45–58.

Pillar, I. and Cho, J. H. (2013). Neoliberalism as Language Policy. *Language in Society*, 42(1), 23–44.

Pitzl, M.-L. (2018). *Creativity in English as a Lingua Franca*. Berlin: Mouton De Gruyter.

Power, M. (1994). *The Audit Explosion*. London: Demos.

Pratt, M. L. (2009). Harm's Way: Language and the contemporary arts of war. *PMLA*, 124(5), 1515–31.

Prodromou, L. (2008). *English as a Lingua Franca: A Corpus-Based Analysis*. London: Continuum.

Purcell, M. 2002. Excavating Lefebvre: The right to the city and its urban politics of the inhabitant. *Geojournal*, 58, 99–108.

Rampton, B. (2006). *Language in Late Modernity*. Cambridge: Cambridge University Press.

Rashith, R. (2012). 'Singlish' video made in US goes viral. 17 December 2012, https://sg.news.yahoo.com/blogs/what-is-buzzing/singlish-video-made-us-goes-viral-071555556.html; accessed 19 May 2020.

Read, J. (2014). The influence of the Common European Framework of Reference (CEFR) in the Asia-Pacific region. *LEARN Journal*, Special issue, 33–9.

Reynolds. S. (2018). 'How Auto-Tune revolutionized the sound of popular music'. Pitchfork.com, 17 September 2018, https://pitchfork.com/features/art icle/how-auto-tune-revolutionized-the-sound-of-popular-music/; accessed 27 January 2021.

Rose, N. (1998). *Inventing Our Selves: Psychology, Power and Personhood*. Cambridge: Cambridge University Press.

Schmid, H.-J. (2020). *The Dynamics of the Linguistic System*. Oxford: Oxford University Press.

Schmidt, R. (1990). The Role of Consciousness in Second Language Learning. *Applied Linguistics*, 11, 129–58.

Schneider, E. W. (2007). *Postcolonial English. Varieties Around the World*. Cambridge: Cambridge University Press.

Schneider, E. W. (2011). English into Asia: From Singaporean Ubiquity to Chinese Learners' Features. In M. Adams and A. Curzan, eds., *Contours of English and English Language Studies*. Ann Arbor: University of Michigan Press, pp. 135–56.

Schneider, E. W. (2014). New Reflections on the Evolutionary Dynamics of World Englishes. *World Englishes*, 33(1), 9–32.

Schneider, E. W. (2020). Calling Englishes as Complex Dynamic Systems: Diffusion and Restructuring. In A. Mauranen and S. Vetchinnikova (eds.), *Language Change: The impact of English as a lingua franca*. Cambridge: Cambridge: University Press, pp. 15–43.

Seargeant, P. (2019). *The Emoji Revolution*. Cambridge: Cambridge University Press.

Seidlhofer, B. (2011). *Understanding English as a Lingua Franca*. Oxford: Oxford University Press.

Silverstein, M. (1996). Monoglot "Standard" in America: Standardization and Metaphors of Linguistic Hegemony. In D. Brenneis and R. K. S. Macaulay, eds., *Matrix of Language: Contemporary linguistic anthropology*. Boulder: Westview, pp. 284–306.

Silverstein, Michael. 2003. Indexical Order and the Dialectics of Sociolinguistic Life. *Language and Communication*, 23, 193–229.

Simmel, G. (1976). *The Metropolis and Mental Life: The sociology of Georg Simmel*. New York: Free Press.

Spolsky, B. (2004). *Language Policy*. Cambridge: Cambridge University Press.

Spolsky, B. (2009). *Language Management*. Cambridge: Cambridge University Press.

Strathern, M., ed. (2000). *Audit Cultures*. London: Routledge.

Stroud, C. and Prinsloo, M. (2015). Preface. In C. Stroud and M. Prinsloo, eds., *Language, Literacy and Diversity: Moving words*. London: Routledge, pp. ix–xiii.

Tollefson, J. (1991). *Planning Language, Planning Inequality*. New York: Longman.

Vertovec, S. (2007). Super-Diversity and its Implications. *Ethnic and Racial Studies*, 30(6), 1024–54.

Vertovec, S. (2010). Towards Post-Multiculturalism? Changing communities, contexts and conditions of diversity. *International Social Science Journal*, 61 (199), 83–95.

Wade, R. H. (2001). Is globalization making world income distribution more equal? *London School of Economics DESTIN Working Paper*, 01–01. London: LSE.

Wee, L. (2003). Linguistic Instrumentalism in Singapore. *Journal of Multilingual and Multicultural Development*, 24(3), 325–38.

Wee, L. (2006). The Semiotics of Language Ideologies in Singapore. *Journal of Sociolinguistics*, 10(3), 344–61.

Wee. L. (2010). Eurasian Singapore English. In D. Schreier, P. Trudgill, E. Schneider and J. Williams, eds., *The Lesser-Known Varieties of English*. Cambridge: Cambridge University Press, pp. 313–326.

Wee, L. (2011). The Ranked List as Panopticon in Enterprise Culture. *Pragmatics and Society*, 2(1), 37–56.

Wee, L. (2018). *The Singlish Controversy: Language, identity and culture in a globalizing world*. Cambridge: Cambridge University Press.

Wee, L. (under preparation). *Automating Language and Communication*.

Widdowson, H. (1994). The Ownership of English. *TESOL Quarterly*, 28(2), 377–89.

Widdowson, H. (2019). Creativity in English. *World Englishes*, 38(1–2), 312–18.

Wiley, T. (1996). Language Planning and Policy. In S. McKay and N. Hornberger, eds., *Sociolinguistics and Language Teaching*. Cambridge: Cambridge University Press, pp. 103–47.

Williams, G. (1992). *Sociolinguistics: A sociological critique*. London: Routledge.

Wise, J.Macgregor (2005). Assemblage. In C. J. Stivale, ed., *Gilles Deleuze: Key concepts*. Montreal/Kingston: McGill and Queen's University Press.

Wittgenstein, L. (1958). *Philosophical Investigations*. Translated by G. E. Anscombe. New York: Macmillan.

Cambridge Elements ≡

World Englishes

Edgar W. Schneider
University of Regensburg
Edgar W. Schneider is Professor Emeritus of English Linguistics at the University of Regensburg, Germany. His many books include *Postcolonial English* (Cambridge, 2007), *English around the World*, 2nd ed. (Cambridge, 2020) and *The Cambridge Handbook of World Englishes* (Cambridge, 2020).

About the Series
Over the last centuries, the English language has spread all over the globe due to a multitude of factors including colonization and globalization. In investigating these phenomena, the vibrant linguistic sub-discipline of "World Englishes" has grown substantially, developing appropriate theoretical frameworks and considering applied issues. This Elements series will cover all the topics of the discipline in an accessible fashion and will be supplemented by online material.

Cambridge Elements ≡

World Englishes

Elements in the Series

Uniformity and Variability in the Indian English Accent
Caroline R. Wiltshire

Posthumanist World Englishes
Lionel Wee

A full series listing is available at: www.cambridge.org/EIWE

Printed in the United States
by Baker & Taylor Publisher Services